THE BOOK OF
BRIXHAM

THE BOOK OF
BRIXHAM

•PORTRAIT OF A HARBOUR TOWN •

FRANK PEARCE

JE MEINTIENDRAY

HALSGROVE

First published in Great Britain in 2000
Reprinted and revised 2002

British Library Cataloguing-in-Publication Data
A CIP record for this title is available from the British Library

ISBN 1 84114 212 3

HALSGROVE
PUBLISHING, MEDIA AND DISTRIBUTION

Halsgrove House
Lower Moor Way
Tiverton, Devon EX16 6SS
Tel: 01884 243242
Fax: 01884 243325
email www.halsgrove.com

Printed and bound in Great Britain by Bookcraft Ltd, Midsomer Norton

Contents

DEDICATION

To my wife Joan
for all her practical support and
infinite encouragement.

Acknowledgements

My sincere appreciation to Dr J. Morgan for his felicitous, esteemed and comprehensive preface. Special thanks to Isabelle Barker for her enthusiasm for the project and as a major contributor of many memorable photographs. Equally so to Mike Thompson of the *Herald Express*, June Disney, David Haddock, Sylvia O'Leary, Joan Longhurst and Ron Weymouth. There have been so many kind people who have contributed in one way or another among whom are: Frank Andrews, J. Banfield, John Charles, Max Danby of Flair Photography, Stan Gregory, E. Hatherleigh, A. Hickman, Albert Hoyle, Danny Irvine, Ray Jago, Mrs D. King, Mr Kralingin (Curator of the Hellevoetsluis Museum), E. Lawrence, E. Mifsud, Peter Malkin, Jack Medland and Mien (the Dutch connection), Jennifer Murray, Derek Pearce, Joy Prowse, John Pike, Mark Poole, Chris and Linda Roach, Brian Slocombe, Savvas Savva, Winnie Snell and daughter Winifred, Mr and Mrs Todd, Edna White and E. Worsfold. Many grateful thanks also for the help given by Torquay Museum and Dr Armitage of Brixham Museum, Terry Harper of the Brixham Cricket Club and the Torquay, Paignton and Brixham libraries. Their support and contributions are greatly appreciated. I am much indebted to the late Arthur C. Ellis' *History of Brixham* from which some information was extracted. My sincere gratitude also to Mr W. Saxton, formerly Town Clerk for many years to the Brixham Town Council for permission to include his Brixham Coat of Arms.

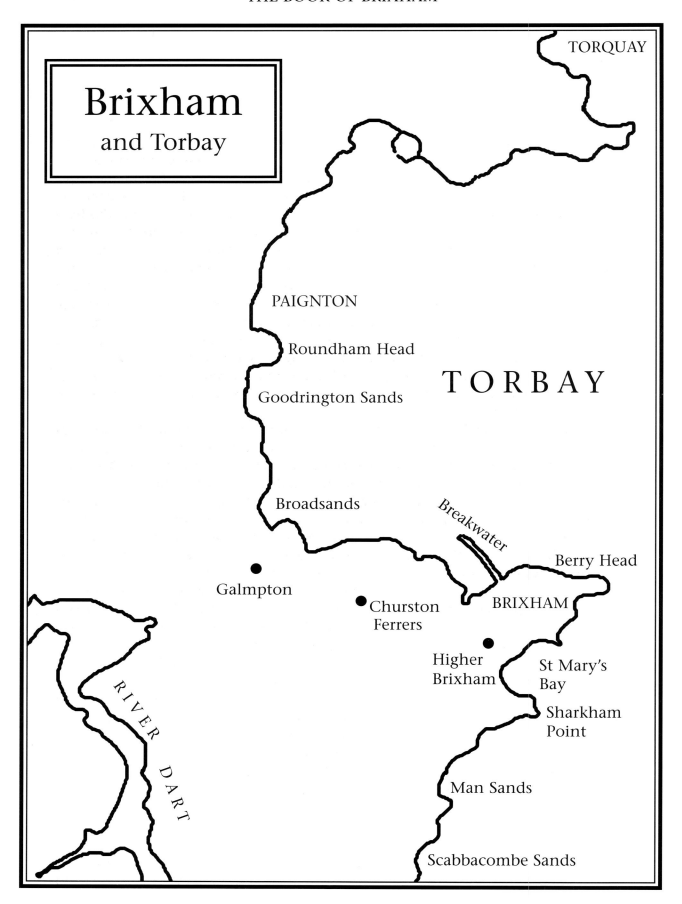

Brixham
and Torbay

TORQUAY

PAIGNTON

Roundham Head

TORBAY

Goodrington Sands

Broadsands

Breakwater

Berry Head

Galmpton

Churston
Ferrers

BRIXHAM

Higher
Brixham

St Mary's
Bay

Sharkham
Point

RIVER DART

Man Sands

Scabbacombe Sands

Foreword

Today few of us write diaries but we have photographs, our own, and those taken by others. They recall past times and, however good, they form in our minds a more vivid and highly sensed picture – as if we had been there. Frank Pearce has written this very special book about Brixham, special because it has a host of memorable photographs, all unique, for the majority are from the personal possessions of Brixham people who have carefully preserved them in prized albums. Proud of their family history they readily responded to Frank's appeal for pictorial contributions to his book: a gesture which was a natural reflection of their liberality. This book, as an attractive illustrated history of the town, should persuade you to again walk around Brixham and acquire a new insight into its past and present. As we pass the old fishmarket towards Fore Street and towards the junction known as Bolton Cross we should remember that long ago it was here the sea reached the shore, and small boats were secured to stout iron rings in the harbour wall. Now, shops hide this wall but behind them the rings may still be seen. Turning left up Bolton Street at the next road crossing we reach the point where stood the Great Gate dividing the fishing village from the farming community (Cowtown) with its 15th century church built on a Saxon site.

If we take the footpath to Berry Head and stand on the higher vantage, there are magnificent views across the Channel towards the French coast. Behind us, where once I walked through wheat fields, the pasture becomes part of the Countryside Park. The steep cliffs here are host to the many seabirds which nest in their thousands. Close by is a searching camera connected to the small Centre high above, enabling pairs of birds at the nesting season to be observed and counted. Apart from this, the moving camera is essential for identifying and describing different birds for the benefit of interested parties of adults and school children. To help these visitors there are, placed within the walls of the Napoleonic fort, reconstructed drawings and diagrams of the buildings as they appeared when in use. The Emperor who evoked such fears of invasion did himself return under very different circumstances, as portrayed in a famous painting. On the decks of HMS *Bellerophon* stands Napoleon fervently searching the shoreline of Torbay with the hope of being granted asylum in our land. Later, the ship with its prisoner turned towards St Helena, an exile from which he never returned. Passing the nearby cliffside hotel, it will be remembered that it was formerly a hospital for the Napoleonic war casualties, but later became the home of the Rev. Francis Lyte. Looking towards a glorious sunset one evening, he was inspired to write the words of the hymn 'Abide With Me'. This solemn hymn was written by a sick man. He left Brixham to seek a drier and warmer climate and arrived at Nice where he lies in the graveyard. I tidied his grave when I was there.

As I write this, fishing trawlers on this calm day are coming home surrounded by a cloud of squawking seagulls. The sea was similarly placid on New Year's Eve in 1915 when battleships were returning from gunnery practice, with HMS *Formidable* last in line, on a course twelve miles south of Berry Head. Near to the fleet was the Brixham trawler *Provident*, skippered by William Pillar. Stalked by a German U-boat, the battleship was struck by a torpedo and quickly began to sink. Even as Pillar rushed to help, a great storm arose. In gale conditions *Provident* eventually reached the sailors in the water, clinging to wreckage. Pillar showed great courage and seamanship by rescuing 72 sailors, and the First Sea Lord at the that time, Winston Churchill, made it his business to see that William Pillar and his crew were rewarded with a sum of money and the silver gallantry medal from the hands of King George V at Buckingham Palace. A year later, the *Provident* itself was torpedoed and sunk, although after the crew had been allowed to leave the ship. Today a similar trawler lies in the harbour, built in 1924 and owned by the Maritime Trust, just one of a number of old wooden trawlers preserved and based at Brixham. With the red-hue of their sails, Brixham harbour is surely their last resting place. Nearby the Torbay Lifeboat swings at her moorings, sharing the harbour with a host of fishing trawlers and ready for any emergency call.

The sea and the people of Brixham have a binding relationship consolidated by tradition and the character of nature. Although they and their families have known hard times and adversity they remain a very kindly and generous people.

Dr J. Morgan
Brixham 2000

Introduction

Cosily nooked on the extremity of a Channel-facing isthmus in beautiful Torbay, and entrenched within the sanctuary of its protective hills, lies the port of Brixham. Justifiably, it has gained the reputation of the 'Friendly Town' and one does not have to be psychic to be conscious of the atmosphere of genuine cordiality and sincerity of welcome radiated by the inhabitants. The town's popularity is undoubtedly attributable to three factors – it is largely unspoilt by the cancer of so-called modern progress, it is a place set apart with a special and unequalled charm, and it remains fundamentally and characteristically Devon.

The present Brixham has grown up around the nucleus of village cottages, all reminders of the days when Brixham was probably the most prosperous fishing port along the coast. The retention of some of its narrow alleyways and quaint stairways, of well-worn steps ascending to jostle with rows of little houses clinging precariously to steep hillsides, amplifies its uniqueness. It is a prospect so dissimilar to the monotonous uniformity of today's housing estates. All roads lead to the busy harbour with its fishing trawlers and a host of private boats, creating an artist's paradise of colour and motion. Brixham is far removed from the atmosphere of so many seaside towns. Here, no juke boxes blast out pop music at maximum volume, or concrete jungles offend the eye.

What it does have however is a measure of composure allied to an atmosphere of substance which makes it special and inimitable, but there is no question of Brixham being retrogressive. On the contrary, the fact that it has a vast number of societies and associations in proportion to the size of its population must make it one of the most active towns in the county. Everyone belongs to something: operatics, bands, choirs, art clubs, floral arrangement groups, football, rugby, swimming, cricket and so on. You name it – Brixham has it. It's not so much a question of what people can do to fill their time, but rather where they can find the time.

The Book of Brixham with its many photographs, reflects not only the history of the town but also its people. Moreover, it reveals an honourable and patriotic past in which kings and queens, princes and princesses, dukes and duchesses have welcomed the opportunity to visit, meet and mingle with the people. Such events are pictorially recorded in the book as a treasured chronicle of the town's history, not only for the present generation, but for the children of the future to enjoy. Many old friends and new have been overwhelmingly kind with their contributions of photographs and information and I sincerely hope that my efforts to faithfully record Brixham's bygone days have justified their confidence in me. There are many to whom I offer my sincere thanks: those who have loaned precious individual photos, albums, newspaper cuttings and anecdotal information which has been of inestimable value. Their contributions have been similar to an encyclopedia of local knowledge which, when added to my own recollections of happy years of residence in Brixham, has given me immense pleasure and satisfaction.

Frank Pearce
2000

A map cartouche showing the landing of the Prince William from his fleet off the coast of Devon 5 November 1688.

1 – Royal Arrivals

While Brixham's ascendancy into the 21st millennium may have been no more dramatic than any other south coast town of its size, its fortune over the last 300 years firmly establishes its place in English history. Prior to the abdication of the throne by the tyrannical James II, at the time that William, Prince of Orange, arrived in Torbay in November 1688 with a great fleet of 500 ships and 15 000 men, it was the people of Brixham who welcomed him with open arms as he stepped ashore on the quay. A copy of a letter dated 1 December 1688, written by one who was with the Prince, and now in the Guildhall Museum, London, states: 'The fleet was a sight of the greatest splendour. There was no opposition for the people bid us heartily welcome, gave us all manner of provisions for our refreshment and welcomed His Highness, the Prince of Orange, with loud acclamations of joy'.

Tradition has it that the Prince said, 'If I am welcome then come and carry me ashore,' whereupon a local fisherman named Varwell plunged into the water and carried him triumphantly to the steps of the pier. Some contend that the story is purely legend for a subsequent account by a certain Thomas Dobbins, Captain and former Gunner of HMS *Nonsuch,* dated 13 February 1693, states 'I am the person who carried the King ashore from his barge and obtained a warrant as Gunner of the *Nonsuch.*'

This seems to have been confirmed by a letter from Sir William Phipps to the Secretary for War, Lord Nottingham, notifying the appointment of Thomas Dobbins as Captain of the *Nonsuch* adding 'He is the same person who carried the King from the barge in Torbay and it was the King's commendation of him that gained him a warrant for being a gunner.'

Receiving such an enthusiastic welcome from the people of Brixham allowed the Prince to secure a bridgehead ashore where his troops encamped and firmly established their position against any surprise attack.

The arrival of the fleet must have presented a scene of spectacular pageantry to the people of Brixham, and to some lesser degree the more distant Paignton and Torquay. A forest of masts and sails would have covered almost the whole of

A portrait of Prince William showing, in the background, the fleet at anchor in Torbay.

Torbay with its capital ships, great men-of-war, fire-ships, smaller gun-ships, frigates, troopships, merchant ships and flyboats. The spectacle would have been further enhanced by each ship's colourful standard flaunting its heraldic coat of arms and its red, white and blue banner indicating its squadron.

Centre stage of all this galaxy of seacraft was the Prince's flagship the *Brill* a new man-of-war of 28 guns flaunting a giant banner displaying the arms of Nassau quartered with those of England and, within this elliptical device, the words of such importance to the people of England 'The Liberties of England and the Protestant Religion' and below them in words three feet high, 'Je Maintiendrai' (I will maintain).

Immediately following the landing, the Prince commanded that a thanksgiving service be held on the beach. It was not just for his officers and nobles but the whole army, participating in the reading of the 118th Psalm, which includes the verse: 'This is the day which the Lord hath made; we will rejoice and be glad in it.'

Following the service, the Prince led a section of his army to the top of the highest hill overlooking the houses, the bay and the surrounding countryside. It must have been an impressive cavalcade for in advance of the main body, led by His Highness, trumpets sounded, fifes and flutes played, drums beat and there was much joyful shouting by the troop of mounted Lords, Knights, noble Gentlemen and Guards bearing their banners of heraldry. It was said that the hurrahs echoed down through the valley to those on the quayside and the crews who remained on the ships.

The simple fisherfolk who led very ordinary mundane lives and who witnessed this ostentatious parade must have been utterly bewildered by what they were seeing, yet with a gladness in their hearts.

That night the Prince slept at one of the fishermen's little cottages while his guards lodged close by. The most credible site for this lodgement is believed to have been in Middle Street (demolished in 1924), which stood opposite the foot of Broad Steps.

On the 6 November orders were given for the army to march towards Exeter via Newton Abbot. Unfortunately, the weather worsened, with torrential rain flooding the dirt roads and lanes. The foot soldiers had no place to sleep save in the thick red clay mud of the fields, sodden in water. In their march towards Newton Abbot, reputed places of meetings and lodgements included Parliament Hill near Marldon, while the Prince himself is believed to have slept one night in Church Street, Paignton, in rooms above what is now known as the Crown and Anchor Inn. The archway is still used to this day by traffic – as a short cut through to Palace Avenue.

The exceptionally bad weather conditions resulted in a large number of troops falling ill and, as there was no hospital in the area, the sick and wounded were brought back to Brixham where the cottagers were implored to each take one or two men and care for them until they recovered. Kindly souls that they were they could hardly refuse such an humanitarian request and, as a result, the former dwellings of Brixham changed almost overnight into individual nursing homes. Apart from the responsibility of tending these sick soldiers they had to be fed, and as time passed the question arose as to how and when was all this was to be paid for.

One can understand the resentment that developed later when after seeking reimbursement from the government for their benevolence and

The obelisk commemorating the landing of William of Orange in Brixham in 1688.

generosity, they were informed that no Act of Parliament existed to oblige them to pay for the nursing care and food the good folk of Brixham had provided. Requests for compensation went on and on, and even eleven years later a petition was sent to Parliament by the poor inhabitants of Brixham, Kingswear and Dartmouth who prayed that the debt of over £1500 for caring for the sick might be paid. The reply was hardly encouraging: 'My Lords will make provision for ye debts relative to ye sick and wounded as soon as they are enabled.' No records exist that the debt was ever repaid.

Later the Prince and his army set off for Exeter, there to establish his headquarters. Having confirmed that most of the country were for him and against James, he advanced to London where he learned that the throne had been vacated by James' flight to France.

Two months later, on the 11 February 1689, William and his wife Mary were solemnly pronounced King and Queen of England. It had been

Brixham from an old drawing of 1830. The foreground is filled by the King's Reservoir built for the navy and in use from 1801. On this site now stands the Town Hall at Bolton Cross. The original All Saints church (Henry Lyte's church) can be seen on the left high ground It was rebuilt after the roof was blown off in the Great Gale of 1866.

a turbulent time for the whole country when the throne of England hung in the balance .

While it may be idle to speculate upon the outcome if William of Orange had received a militant reception at Brixham, the fact remains that there would undoubtedly have been bloodshed, which in turn would have inflamed the country. The anger emerging from this would have played right into the hands of James, eventually opening the way for a Papal State dictated by Rome. Thus it can be seen, it was only by the initial welcoming hand of friendship by the 6000 inhabitants of Brixham that the destiny of the English throne was preserved. It can be said that this was a typical example of the truism that 'small events are a part of larger events, each sending out ripples over the ocean of years.'

THE KING'S RESERVOIR

In the 18th and 19th century there was a reservoir in Brixham which served ships of the King's fleet when in the shelter of Torbay. A letter dated March 1672, written by one Richard Cliffe to the Navy Office at Trinity House, London, reads as follows:

To the Right Honourable —
...and I doe finde that good conviencyes may be made for ye supplying his Majesties shipps and

fleetes with good water as oftime as their ocations may require the same... and their is a large poole made to receive the same.
Your honoured and humble servant,
Richard Cliffe, Brixham, 1672

Torbay was a haven of refuge in those days to which the fleet had frequent occasion to resort. Although the actual position of that pool is uncertain, it is known that in 1801 the Government constructed a large reservoir known as the King's Reservoir on the site of the present Town Hall. Water was piped down to the quay to enable warships and other vessels to water quickly.

During excavations before the Second World War, while laying a new gas main outside the library, a section of a wooden conduit was found, believed to be one of the original pipes made of elm.

THE KING'S STATUE

On Brixham quay, overlooking the harbour, stands an imposing statue of William, Prince of Orange. It reminds visitors and the town's inhabitants of the part Brixham played in welcoming the man who rose up to restore the liberties of England and the Protestant religion.

Two hundred years later, on the 5 November 1888 the foundation stone of the pedestal for a

Crowds gather before the statue of William of Orange on one of the many celebratory occasions in Brixham commemorating his landing in 1688. This photograph was taken in 1950.

monument to his memory was laid by Count Van Bylandt, the ambassador representing the Netherlands.

Accepting a silver trowel presented for the occasion, Count Van Bylandt proclaimed 'I declare this foundation stone of the proposed monument to be laid, in the name of my Royal master the King of the Netherlands, and allow me to add, in the name of the British nation, the loyal people of a great country.'

The statue was finally unveiled on the 5 November, 1889. Mounted on a 10 feet high granite pedestal the 8 feet high effigy, weighing two tons, depicts William with his right foot on a rock his right hand holding his plumed hat and his left hand on his heart.

2 – Early Days

In the 18th century, Torbay was frequently used and visited by the Royal Navy's Channel Fleet under the command of Admiral Lord Howe. A report dated 1794 states that he spent one or two nights at numbers 24 and 26 Middle Street, Brixham, which was at that time one house. In those days Torbay was a safe and convenient haven for the English fleet for from here they could sail out to pounce upon enemy ships venturing up or down the Channel. In that same year Lord Howe's ships lay off Brixham for over three months before weighing anchor. Their long stay prompted the waggish locals to remark: 'If they don't move soon they'll go aground on all the beef bones they've been throwing overboard.'

THE GREAT GALE

As mentioned in the previous chapter, the Great Gale of 1866 caused enormous damage in the town. It blew the roof off All Saint's church and

Above: *Brixham harbour from a drawing dated 1825.* Top right: *Middle Street, Brixham, in the 1880s.*

Right: *Wooden sailing vessels lean crazily against the harbour wall following the Great Gale of 1866.*

Below: *Stricken ships lie amid the flotsam following the Great Gale. It was said it was possible to walk dryshod across the harbour on the floating timber.*

created havoc among the fishing fleet in the harbour. Vessels were destroyed and many trawler owners went bankrupt. The photographs shown here indicate the ferocity of the gale inside what is a safe anchorage.

SMUGGLING DAYS

The constant war against France caused a great drain upon the financial resources of England and measures were taken to balance the books by the introduction of what was known as the Smuggler's Act, when it was deemed a crime to import certain goods without paying tax, among which were brandy, tobacco and tea. The introduction of this levy by the faceless authorities in Parliament was cruel enough, but when the government of the day established customs houses and employed revenue men, including searchers, custom's officers crews and preventive men to implement the law, it inflamed opinion throughout the country.

Especially under threat were those who operated the brandy runs from Roskoff and St Malo in France from which a nice little income was made to supplement their meagre earnings from fishing. The application of the Act affected them greatly and most were determined to flout the new law come what may. Thus the smuggler was born creating a history over 200 years of secret

meetings, landings by night, skirmishes ashore, fights on cliffs, and the hidden storage of kegs of brandy in many a lonely cove along the coast. In fact the whole coastline from Durl Head through St Mary's Bay to Sharkham Point and on to Man Sands were constantly used as off-loading points.

Once close to shore, the illegal kegs would be lowered to the sea-bed with stones attached and long ropes secured to floats. After dark, the barrels would be collected and taken ashore where the runners would be waiting to take them inland

Left: *Enclosed and sheltered Fishcombe Cove in St Mary's Bay was an ideal location for smugglers. Churston Quay can be seen in the background.*

Below: *Another view of St Mary's Bay.*

to taverns or as they were called in those far off days, kiddly-winks.

Experience of fluctuation in tides sometimes meant that kegs could be thrown overboard in the dark, some way offshore, and allowed to float in to certain little coves and there picked up.

Smugglers would of course operate at night during the darkest hours and, if they had to travel through little hamlets and villages, it is said they would sometimes dress up in white sheets to keep the superstitious and gullible villagers away from doors and windows. Most people however knew what was going on and there was often a sense of loyalty towards the smugglers. In his poem 'The Smuggler's Song' Rudyard Kipling wonderfully evokes the spirit of those times:

> *Five and twenty ponies walkin' through the dark,*
> *Brandy for the Parson, Baccy for the Clerk,*
> *Laces for a lady, letters for a spy;*
> *So watch the wall my darling while the gentlemen*
> *go by.*

The smuggler's fast sailing boats would set off from Start Point, only about a hundred miles from the Brittany ports of St Malo and Roskoff where the kegs of best French brandy could be bought and loaded. Most of the smuggling boats returned at night, but if by day they had col-

leagues ashore who would give warning signals that the Revenue officers were about. When the kegs of brandy were landed, teams of men called runners would be ready with ponies. A runner had two ponies, one to ride and one to lead, with each pony carrying two kegs of brandy. A runner was paid one shilling per night, and if the run was entirely successful, a further five shillings.

Mistakes and miscalculations were of course bound to happen however careful the planning, and there were occasions when the Revenue men would be waiting on shore for them. Sometimes, to avoid capture, the smugglers would shave the ponies' tails and manes and cover them all over with thick grease to make them too slippery to hold.

Extraordinary measures were also made to conceal the contraband spirits. On the boats themselves, timbers were hollowed out, innocent water casks were divided into two or three sections, one holding the spirits.

Sometimes the returning smugglers' boats would be intercepted offshore by the custom's men in their fast cutters and the boat searched. Rarely was anything unlawful found for the brandy kegs were often suspended under the keel and towed all the way back to one of their secret landing coves between Sharkham Point and Man Sands, Churston and Fishcombe.

A view of the fortifications at Berry Head showing the entrance, once protected by a drawbridge.

A lighthouse keeper leans on the railings outside the old powder store, now part of the lighthouse complex at Berry Head. This photograph dates from around 1900.

3 – Berry Head

Towards the close of the 18th century Britain's military commitments were prodigious. Thousands of troops served overseas in places such as India, Gibraltar, Australia, New Zealand, and the West Indies. Support for these overseas contingents rested on fleet transport and armed ships to accompany them. At one time in Torbay there were 344 ships, including armed support, lying ready to sail. Fleets awaiting orders in weather-protected Torbay had to be revictualled every six weeks and Brixham harbour became the main station of supply. After receiving food allocations the ships were towed across the harbour to receive their water supply from the reservoir built for this purpose.

Throughout the time the fleet were in Torbay with their sails down, they were of course vulnerable to attack and so the defence of this southern port became of utmost importance. The earliest reference to a definite defence of Berry Head appears to have been made in 1779, recording that 'Berry Head should be armed as the most secure road for shipping and not an unlikely place for the enemy to land.' It was in this year that land was leased and gun positions established, with militia and regular troops stationed at Berry Head and nearby Battery Gardens.

When France declared war in 1793, the British government decided to further fortify Torbay and 28 acres of land were purchased on Berry Head in 1794. Several wooden huts were built and occupied by troops. The basic plan called for guns to defend the harbour and forts to defend the guns from land attack. The estimated cost, even in those days, was a massive £30 595.00, and the contractor, strangely enough, was a woman, Mrs Susanna Croed.

By 1801, records show that a total of 448 soldiers were stationed here and, following the renewal of war with France, a contract was signed for the erection of new barracks in 1803 which were ready for occupation in 1805. The first regiment in the new forts was the Dorset militia followed by militia from Devon, Somerset, Berkshire and Cornwall.

Plans at the War Office show that No.1 Fort was defended by eight 24-pounders with one barracks building, while the much larger No.3 barracks, at the seaward or eastern end, had twelve 24-pounders, each weighing over three tons. In the north-west corner were three 24-pounders, eight barracks in all with a kitchen to each. Additionally, each fort had its guard house, magazines, storehouses, officers' mess etc.

Gunnery drill on a 7-inch 110-pounder on a traversing siege carriage, c.1880.

Berry Head lighthouse, 1906.

In 1859 there was fear that Britain might become involved in another war with France and, as a result, a local volunteer force, the Royal Sea Fencibles, was formed on the rumour that French ships entering Torbay were considering a plan to occupy the peninsular embracing Brixham and Churston. The French scheme, they thought, involved digging a huge strongly-fortified trench stretching from an arm of the river Dart (Galmpton Creek) to the south-west corner (Broadsands) across Galmpton to Warborough. When the sea flowed through from both directions the trench would create a canal from which they could form a defensive position, going on then to conquer England. However, this madcap plan never materialised.

In more recent years, Berry Head has been used as a battery for the Royal Naval Reserve and as a Coastguard Station. It was the second largest station in England with some 700 men being trained here annually until the outbreak of the Second World War. It has also been used by the Brixham Sea Scouts and as a Lloyd's Signalling Station.

Close by are foundations of the old hospital, in use from 1803 to 1809. The present lighthouse incorporates these buildings and dates from 1905 and, although squat in appearance, the light is actually nearly two hundred feet above sea level and a double flash is projected over a radius of twenty miles at intervals of fifteen seconds. The old powder magazine is used as a watch tower and signal station.

The approach to the fort is by a bridge (originally a drawbridge over a dry moat formerly studded with spikes and entanglements).

Throughout these periods of threatened invasion Brixham must have often provided a colourful spectacle. It was then the nearest place to Brest and St Malo where the fleets could shelter from the westerly gales, adding to the garrison or to the town another 2500 sailors. At such times the streets must have swarmed with sailors and marines, in addition to the scarlet-coated soldiers from Berry Head. At this time Brixham was the largest settlement in the bay and an important naval base. By comparison Brixham's resident population was 1671 while that of Torre and Torquay was only 838.

Berry Head forts were dismantled in 1817 and by 1832 there remained only the shell of its former habitation. Nearly two centuries have passed since the captains and the troops withdrew and the clamour of its roads fell silent. Now no bugle calls disturb the rambling paths, no tramping feet employ the open ways, no soldiers quick of oath and raucous song pervade the barrack halls, all these have gone. Instead great swarms of seagulls swoop and scream at tourists while, close by, a white-haired gardener tends his favoured cabbage plot.

4 – Abide With Me

Close to the forts at Berry Head stands Berry Head House, built during 1806–1809 as a hospital but seemingly never occupied as such, and in 1832 the Rev H.F. Lyte took up his residence there. Later it was purchased by his curate and son-in-law, the Rev J.R. Hogg, while Lyte continued to live there rent free.

The postcard shown below commemorates the Reverend Henry Francis Lyte, author of the the famous hymn 'Abide With Me'. On the left is depicted the church where he preached and on the right Berry Head House.

The family of the Rev Hogg lived at Berry Head House for many years, the last representative being his third daughter Miss A.M. Hogg who had been a lady-in-waiting to Queen Victoria and who came to live here on the death of her sisters. It was she who bought Berry Head from the Government in 1886. In 1895 Miss Hogg gave to the Urban District Council the right of using the paths on the Head in perpetuity so that it might always be open to the public. After being bedridden for some time Miss Hogg died in December 1933.

After her death the Council thought the time had come to negotiate for the purchase of the headland and made a tentative proposal offering £9000 to the Trustees for the 196 acres. The Trustees however, countered with a demand for £30 000, or an alternative offer on conditions which later proved to be unacceptable. The Trustees then launched a plan to build houses over the land at six to the acre. This was successfully repulsed in 1934. Over the years there were many arbitrary meetings and heated discussions between interested parties which were finally settled with the ownership of the land being safely transferred into the hands of the Torbay Council.

THE CENTENARY OF HENRY FRANCIS LYTE.
1793–1847

The commemoration of the centenary of Henry Francis Lyte of Brixham took place at St Margaret's, Westminster on 23 November, 1947. In Brixham, some 150 people attended a memorial gathering outside Berry Head House

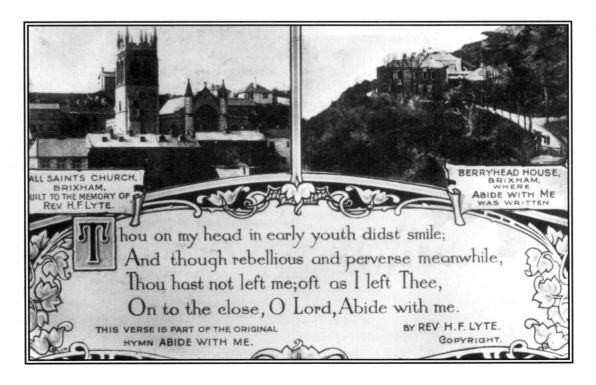

The Rev. Henry Francis Lyte.

where at one time Francis Lyte lived. The singing was led by the Salvation Army Band and their choristers singing the hymn 'Abide With Me'. That evening a joint Scottish–Brixham broadcast took place with a sermon by the Dean of Exeter, the Very Rev. S.C. Carpenter, the service also concluding with the famous hymn. It was attended by the Chairman and members of the U.D.C together with members of the Lyte family and all the clergy and ministers of Brixham.

The people of Brixham should be justly proud of their town's association with this great man. In any event, the inhabitants are frequently reminded by the carillon of chimes from the central church of All Saints pealing the first few notes of Lyte's immortal hymn.

Left and below: *Berry Head house, home of the Rev. Henry Francis Lyte. The postcard image below shows the spectacular location of the house overlooking the sea.*

5 – Churston Ferrers

The name Ferrers is derived from the 13th century family of Sir Hugh Ferrers and the village is a ward of the town of Brixham. This charming little place has a rurality all its own for by its singular position it is neither insular nor urban. Although lying aslant the busy main thoroughfare into Brixham it remains impassively detached, happily content with the aura of its anonymity. A few excellent but unpretentious residences lie cheek-by-jowl with their cottage counterparts of another age, all jealously guarding the unique character of their tranquil existence.

The village is justifiably proud of its enchanting Churston Court Inn of Saxon Manor vintage for here the Saxon Earl Ulf and his son Judhael lived as Lords of Totnes and all the surrounding lands in the first half of the 11th century. Its importance is also evidenced by its pictorial representation on the Mayor of Torbay's chain of office.

Following the Norman Conquest the Court was inherited by the order of the monks of Totnes and it is said that the ghost of a monk, hooded and gowned, appears as a shadowy figure from time-to-time before melting away into the substance of the inn's ancient walls. Others have experienced seeing table glasses mysteriously move, and candles that light of their own accord!

Later in its long history, it became a manor to Sir Hugh Ferrers and his family. Even in the reign of Good Queen Bess it was an inn, and sea captains anchored their ships in Churston Cove, arriving at the inn via an old underground passage. One of these captains was the famous Sir Humphrey Gilbert who colonised Newfoundland and who lived barely a mile away at Greenaway. Later he, with his half-brother Sir Walter Ralegh, fought the great galleons of the Spanish Armada off the coast of England.

The interior of the inn is richly endowed with history. A labyrinth of corridors give access to small dining chambers each with ample evidence of bygone days. Original mullioned windows, oak beamed ceilings, and ancient fireplaces with carved surrounds date back to 1721.

Churston Ferrers School, 1913

Churston Court and the age old village of Churston Ferrers, each complimentary to the other, have dwelt together for many centuries. Over the years it has seen the passing of the great and famous and in more recent times the writer Agatha Christie often stayed here, while at the other end of the notoriety, Bruce Reynolds hid at Churston Court after his part in the Great Train Robbery of 1963.

Churston Court Inn.

Churston Ferrers – a view in 1912.

6 – Fishing and Fishermen

Nearly eighty years ago a certain Mary E. Fraser, so enchanted and charmed by the town of Brixham wrote the following lines which were published in the Town Guide.

Now Brixham sits around her quay
In tiers of quaint old houses,
A' watching o'er the changeful sea
Lest storm its passion rouses
Against the gallant boats that ride
With brown sails set and nets flung wide,
For the fish that feed
The brain and breed
That make Heaven
Of Devon
And Brixham.

At the beginning of the 19th century, Brixham supplied the fishmarkets of London, Bristol, Bath and Exeter. One writer of the period described Brixham in these terms: 'An extensive fishery is carried on at Brixham for turbot, sole, whiting, mackerel etc, etc. The Bath and Exeter markets are supplied from this place and great quantities sent to London, being conveyed by water to Portsmouth and thence by land. About 100 trawlers are employed in the fishery. The estimated value is £80 000 per year.'

There is no doubt that at one time, Brixham headed all other coastal towns as the most successful fishing port in England. Around the 1830s another writer observed: 'Brixham has often been described as the Mother of Deep Sea Fishing with its brown sail trawlers reaping the harvest of its coastal and channel waters. This was in no small part consequent upon the decline of the Dutch fishing industry attributable to the Napoleonic wars which in turn enabled the men of Brixham in 1815 to introduce trawling into Dover and Ramsgate from whence it extended to Yarmouth, Scarborough, Hull, Harwich, Lowestoft and Grimsby. It thus established the foundation of an enormous trade, with trawling becoming the

Brixham trawlers waiting for a breeze. The suggested date of this view is 1868.

Left and below: *Brixham's fishing fleet in harbour during the 1880s.*

Left: *Net mending on the quayside.*

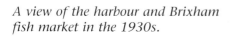

A view of the harbour and Brixham fish market in the 1930s.

Above: Wooden sailing vessels lie against the harbour wall, with the dark sails of the fishing fleet seen beyond, in 1912. Below: Brixham fisherman on board their trawler.

most important branch of fishing, as by this method, the choicest fish were caught.'

As time passed and with the advent of the steam-trawler, the fishing industry spread its nets into more distant waters, from the White Sea in the north to the coast of Morocco in the south.

One of the best-known retail fish firms in Brixham was Banfield & Son which was founded in 1841. In those days, soles sold at threepence a pound, turbot and brill at twopence, and rays given to the poor three times a week.

Through relays of horses, fish had to be taken to Bristol by road and it was not until the Brixham and Churston railway was constructed that fish could be sent to London and provincial markets. By the 1850s, it was claimed that Brixham had the largest fishery in England with 276 'sail of vessels' ranging from 30 to 180 tons comprising 20 000 tons of shipping and employing 1500 men with about 350 tons weight of fish producing £600 per week.

In 1870 Brixham fisheries hit a 'boom time', more by accident than any other reason. At this period, Brixham fleets had confined their activities within a sea limit of some 20 miles. But four more adventurous trawlers had been trawling in the North Sea and selling their catches at Scarborough. One of the four, who had been fish-

Right: Terminus, *the last trawlers to be built at Jackman's Breakwater shipyard in 1911.*

Below: *The men who helped to build the* Terminus.

Right: Jackman's *shipyard in 1880.*

ing off the Dogger Bank in the North Sea had a catch of very fine sole in the fishing ground later known as the 'Silver Pits'. Fearful of a brewing storm, he sailed into Hull where at that time there was no regular market for fish. So successful was the enterprise that by the following year a fleet of seven Brixham smacks, sailed for the 'Silver Pits' thus opening up a highly successful market opportunity.

Brixham Fisheries were now on the crest of a financial wave. So vibrant was the industry that a commercial fever swept the town. There was a stampede to buy shares in the fishing fleet and the building of new trawlers also flourished. Householders even sold their houses or borrowed money in their eagerness to make a fortune from the highly profitable fish trade. By 1877 Brixham gained the reputation of being the wealthiest

An interesting array of working gear is on display in this marvellous photograph of Brixham fishermen. Below: men aboard trawler BM316.

town of its size on the English Channel. As one old wag was heard to remark 'Its the best *plaice* in England!'.

As time passed, larger and more powerful fleets came into being, not just for Brixham but for Grimsby, Lowestoft and Hull, with especially the last named developing into a successful and regular landing place for the quality catches. The absence of a rail system at Brixham for the transportation of their fish to large markets in London and Bath was an unsatisfactory element in an otherwise prosperous enterprise.

The establishment of a rail link came about through a totally unexpected event when substantial deposits of iron ore were discovered at Furseham by R.W. Wolston and Dr Calley. Due to the enterprise of the former, a line to Brixham from Churston station was constructed and opened for goods traffic in 1869, putting Brixham within a few hours of Billingsgate fish market and on a competitive footing with Hull. By 1883 the Brixham company sold its interest in the line which was then taken over by the Great Western Railway.

With the advantage of the introduction of steam trawlers, as opposed to those reliant on sail, by the year 1888 2600 tons of fish were sent from Brixham to London annually. So flourishing was

trade that every fisherman's ambition was to own his own trawler and there were occasions, when all boats were back from the sea, that it was possible to walk from vessel to vessel from one side of the harbour to the other.

After decades of holding a prime position in the country's fishing trade Brixham as a leading fishing port slid into decline with the outbreak of the 1914–1918 war. An Admiralty ban on fishing in certain areas saw catches plummet. These restrictions were to occur again in 1947 when the Admiralty placed a ban on fishing in Lyme Bay due to bombing practice. Protests were frequent and vociferous but eventually and after a stormy meeting in 1951 between the Ministry of Supply, the RAF and various fishing bodies it was agreed to allow fishing to continue.

For almost two hundred years the port has thrived through its fishing fleet. Over many generations the call of the sea has shaped the course and career of thousands of Brixham fathers and sons. Despite the knowledge that the profession is one of the most dangerous, their love of the sea transcended all other considerations.

Views of Brixham's fishing heritage:

Right: *Mending nets in Pump Lane.*

Below: *Loading fish into barrels on fish market day in the 1960s.*

Bottom: *A busy quayside scene at Brixham fish market in the 1950s; note the wooden barrels compared with those made of aluminium in the more recent photograph.*

7 – Regatta

Doubtless all Brixham people would agree that the most exciting event of Regatta Week is the local Trawler Race which takes place usually at the end of August. Above is a rare photograph of the crew of the *Ebenezer* which competed in the Brixham Regatta race of 1910. Among those who can be identified are C. Perrett, Foster, Lane Snr, Lane Jnr, Moore, H. Hatherley, F. Hatherley, T. Jackman, G. Webber, H. Worth, R. Ansell, and the owner Tom Adams in the front row, second from left. The race encompassed a three times circuit of a course from the starting buoy off Battery Point via Goodrington, around the Orestone off Torquay, and back to Battery Point.

Above: *Regatta day in Brixham 1910 with all the fun of the fair. One booth advertises 'Egyptian Mysteries'.*
Right: *Donkey rides at the fair.*

8 – Late Victorian & Edwardian Brixham

The death of Queen Victoria in 1901 ushered in an entirely new a way of life to that experienced in the Victorian Age. The dawn of the new era, with Edward VII occupying the throne, forced people to reflect on the previous century, a time when the country was at the heart of the greatest Empire the world had known. In the uncertainty of the future could Britain advance or even maintain her successes or would there be change?

Between 1910 and 1914 the dark clouds of a pending war were steadily gathering over Europe. Here major countries constantly argued, demanding room for expansion, and on several occasions were on the brink of war. Germany was the prime mover in these threatening times instigated by its leader Kaiser Wilhelm. The main sabre-rattling from Germany was directed against their neighbour, Russia, but soon each of the major countries made plans for general mobilization, accepting that war was inevitable.

The expansion of Germany's army and particularly her navy imposed a serious threat to Britain's seapower on which, she as an island, was utterly dependent.

Victoria's reign had firmly established the nation as the undisputed leader in all the areas of civilised endeavour: invention, science, literature, architecture, transport and engineering. But as the years of the new century passed all was not well at home. The rise of trade unionism, strikes, the emergence of the Suffragette movement, all indicated that the country was sailing into less calm waters.

There were however, compensatory developments – Marconi's first transatlantic wireless message from Newfoundland to Cornwall in 1901; Britain's launching of her first submarine; the ending of the Boer War 1902; and the first successful air flight by the Wright brothers in 1903.

The motor-car was, by 1905, a familiar sight on the streets of London, slowly replacing the horse-drawn cab, and it wasn't long before the streets of Brixham had to accept this fast-moving transition to modern technology.

Above: *A rare photograph of construction work in the building of the breakwater in 1908.*

Opposite page clockwise from top left: *1. The lower end of Middle Street c.1900. 2. The old water supply at St Mary's Square, with St Mary's church in the background, 1906 3. A Brixham street 'bit' in 1908. The Tribble family at the celebration of the Coronation of Edward VII in 1901.*

Above left: *The end of Higher Street, leading to Furzeham, in 1912, now demolished.* Above right: *Fishermen's wives meet at the steps leading to Prospect Road, 1902.*

A day out on Mudstone beach in 1908 included pony rides. Seaside excursions were now growing in popularity and developing motor transport and railways made day trips a feasible proposition.

Pleasure boats also grew in popularity in the early years of the 20th century, with steamers calling in at various ports, or taking passengers on round trips. Here well-dressed passengers from the pleasure boat *Pioneer* disembark at Brixham Harbour, 1909.

The higher part of Middle Street in 1914. Note the solitary car - precursor of many. History records that William Prince of Orange stayed at the second house on the right.

A celebration parade in Brixham's town centre marking the coronation of King George V in 1911.

A Brixham Scout group of 1914. Baden Powell's initiative was relatively recent at this time but boys were encouraged to act in a soldierly manner — and many were to fight and die in the Great War. Shown here left to right are: Dick Clark, Eric Lever, Harold Dewdney, Gerald Bridgeman, Reg Smardon, and Patrol Leader Harry Gowman.

It is 1914 and the Medland family set out in their wagonette for Shaugh Bridge. The driver, Sonny Baker, enlisted the day after this photograph was taken and was later killed in the Great War

The name Pillar was synonymous was heroism during the Great War. Here, in 1915, John Pillar skippers the pilot boat Mellrose registered in both Brixham and Dartmouth. This vessel did much sterling work in on anti-submarine patrols off the Devon coast.

9 – The Great War Period

The advent of the Great War, glibly called 'The War to end all Wars', had a mixed reception in Britain; men cheered, women feared, patriotism soared. It was a war engineered by Kaiser Wilhelm (a grandson of England's Queen Victoria) who was determined to have war and went to extreme measures to promote it. In England, a wave of willingness to be prepared to die for King and Country was enthusiastically stimulated by both national newspapers and some politicians.

For many, the call to arms was a call of adventure, an opportunity to perform deeds of heroism, and perhaps to escape from poverty and boredom at home. However, a few weeks in the mud and blood of the trenches of France while German guns wiped out whole battalions of infantry later changed that. The newspapers' predictions that it would all be over by Christmas 1914 was proved ill-founded, as the war dragged on for four ghastly years with millions being killed or wounded.

To say that Britain was unprepared for such a military engagement is a massive understatement, a situation that was to be repeated 25 years later in 1939. The war of 1914–1918 cast a mournful spell over the whole nation.

However, it was also a period of technological development. The arrival of electric power into more and more homes meant, literally, that new light was thrown on the domestic world. Long before television, home entertainment was provided by the family and, once every three or four weeks, a popular Sunday newspaper would include sheet music for a new song which the family would learn to play and sing. Some of these Great War songs also became popular at the Front and helped to keep up morale.

Early in the war fishing became seriously disrupted by the restrictions placed on boats entering sea lanes proscribed by the Admiralty. Only when fishing catches dropped dramatically were the authorities persuaded to allow trawlers back on to their old ground. There was a shortage of young men to man the boats and the traditional roles undertaken by women back on the quayside fell more heavily on their shoulders, along with many other tasks associated with 'War Work'.

By the war's end a terrible toll had been taken on the lives of serving men, while the Spanish Flu

The Home Fleet in Torbay, early in 1914, provides a dazzling searchlight display.

epidemic was felt particularly severely among the impoverished and undernourished people of Devon. In the years following the war national unemployment soared to well over a million and it became a familiar sight to see bemedalled soldiers standing at street corners begging for pennies. Ex-soldiers became itinerant vendors wandering the lanes and back streets with such cries as 'Fresh 'ake, mackerel and whiting' or 'Any rags, bottles or bones.' The Salvation Army 'soup kitchen' was often the only thing that stood between them and starvation.

Even so, for lucky children who might have a Saturday penny, the sweet shop was an earthly paradise. Liquorice laces and gelatine lozenges were an irresistible temptation, as were marbled gob-stoppers and spearmint whirls, temporarily resident in tall gleaming glass jars. Toffee came in slabs in shallow trays to be broken into pieces by a small toffee-hammer by the shopkeeper, bringing mouth-watering anticipation. At railway stations, vending machines dispensed Cadbury's and Fry's chocolate bars for twopence.

But poverty was manifest in the home, on the streets and in every walk of life, and hand-in-hand came poor sanitation and bad housing. A malaise of disaffection and bitterness existed throughout the country. This was reflected in strikes on the railways, trams, shipyards, docks and coalmines. The aftermath of the war was a bleak time for everyone.

Left: *During the Great War land at Berry Head was used by the Royal Navy for training exercises. These men are practising firing rockets.*

Below: *Furzeham in 1915. The Green is being cultivated by Furzeham schoolboys in order to grow food for the local populace. At this time none of the houses which now line the green had been built.*

Below: *The Great War saw an increase in all types of motorised transport. Here, in 1916, a charabanc plies between Paignton, Churston and Brixham.*

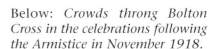

Below: *Crowds throng Bolton Cross in the celebrations following the Armistice in November 1918.*

10 – Into the Twenties

Although the Great War brought little in the way benefit to the people of Brixham the pace of technological change did bring some improvement into their lives. More and more trawlers were to be fitted with engines thus enabling skippers to take their vessels into new fishing grounds. It also made such trips safer, for no longer were they at the mercy of tide and weather.

Motor transport and the railway meant that people could travel further afield, and communication with the outside world brought, albeit imperceptibly, social changes that were to be fundamental.

Up to the 1920s, wireless was practically unknown, at least to the general public, but in 1923 an article appeared in the magazine *Boy's Own* on how to build a wireless set. Requirements were a small wooden board, some copper wire, a 'cat's whisker', a crystal, and a pair of earphones. When he was 14 years old Brian Dibley recalls how his parents were convinced of the absurdity of spending money on such a crazy idea. 'Of course, he'll never hear anything,' they said, 'but at least it'll keep him quiet.' Having assembled these parts, the family were utterly astonished when through the earphones a voice announced 'This is 2LO London calling.' They were actually hearing a voice from over 200 miles away without a telephone connection. The miracle of the century had arrived. The modern world would rename it 'radio' but to the older generation it would always be the 'wireless'.

For the first time too, the Great War had seen the development of cinema. First newsreels brought flickering images of the war on the Western Front, and silent films from America brought people flocking to their local picture house. The first known cinema in Brixham was the 'Electric', owned by the Ellis family, and seating 500 people.

Although not without charm the older houses of Brixham were often in poor condition and unsanitary. This photograph, of Overgang, was taken in 1921.

Something of the poor condition of the town immediately following the Great War can be gauged from this photograph of a 'bit' leading directly on to the quay, taken in 1920.

Above: *The importance of the bicycle in providing an opportunity for independence should not be overlooked and many cycling clubs sprang up in the years before and after the Great War. This cyclist poses in Bolton Cross, 1908.*

Right: *A little gang of children sit outside the New Quay Inn, known locally as 'The Hole in the Wall.'*

Left: *The railway transformed Brixham, both as a commercial port and insofar as it provided a cheap means of transport for its inhabitants.*

Below: *Bolton Cross in 1922. The sight of motor cars in the street no longer turned heads while the old drinking trough was soon to become redundant.*

Below: *The tea rooms at Berry Head catered for the growing numbers of visitors to Brixham and the other Torbay towns. Tourism was soon to became a staple of the local economy.*

Below: *A light fall of snow decorates Middle Street in the 1920s. Inset below: An unknown Brixham family gather in front of their cottage. Note the weatherboard walls.*

These two photographs, the top one taken around the time of the Great War and the lower photograph in 1925, reflect the rapid change from a tranquil scene of sailing vessels to the bustle of a busy Fore Street where cars easily outnumber horse-drawn vehicles.

11 – The Lifeboat

Prior to 1866 the nearest lifeboat available to assist Torbay was at Teignmouth which in any great storm had to be horse drawn to Torquay and launched from the Strand. By the autumn of 1867 however, a lifeboat named *City of Exeter,* subscribed to by the city of Exeter and well supported by local contributions, was launched. The boat was kept at Bolton Cross close to the site of the present-day Conservative Club, just outside the wall of the naval reservoir, and from here it had to be drawn down Fore Street to be launched from the old slipway. This boat was replaced in 1885 by the *Brian Bates* and later, in 1894, the *Betsy Newbon* which in her many years' service saved 109 lives.

A new boat arrived in 1922, the *Alfred and Clara Heath* which in eight years of valiant rescues saved over sixty-four lives, but in September 1930 she in turn was replaced by a new vessel, the finest launched to date, having two 60hp engines and capable of making 9 knots with capacity to carry a hundred people. Her tanks could hold 160 gallons of petrol and produce a fast cruising speed for 16 hours. Practically unsinkable, she had eight watertight compartments and 160 air cases.

She was later named in honour of Sir George Shee, Secretary of the RNLI from 1910 to 1931, and in appreciation of his long service. When asked to present a boat to one of six possible places he chose Brixham, as a compliment to the outstanding seamanship of its lifeboatmen.

At this time the Prince of Wales (later Duke of Windsor) was President of the RNLI and the local Secretary H.M. Smardon proposed that his Royal Highness should be invited to officially launch the new lifeboat. The township of Brixham felt honoured indeed when the Prince consented to do this and Mr Smardon was asked to undertake arrangements for the visit.

On the 27 July, 1932, the Prince lunched at Lupton House with Lord Churston, Bishop Cecil of Exeter, Lord Mildmay, Sir Godfrey Baring and Sir George Shee.

Of the many awards and commendations won by lifeboatmen of Brixham just a few are mentioned here. On the 6 May 1936, the Duke of Kent, as President of the RNLI, presented to coxswain W.H.H. Mugridge the Bronze Medal of the Institution, with other awards to crew members. Three years later, in 1939 a silver medal was presented to coxswain Mugridge with further awards to each crew member.

Among the records up to 1952, it is recorded that after 34 years with the lifeboat, Coxswain Sanders resigned his position for health reasons. At that time the Torbay lifeboat operating from Brixham had saved a total of 392 lives of which 92 were rescued under his direction.

Some of the crew of the Brixham lifeboat in 1936, including Bill Pillar and Bill Mugridge, with H.M. Smardon.

A group of happy flag-sellers in Brixham raising money for the RNLI in the 1930s.

Lifeboatmen Bill Mugridge and Bill Pillar c.1935.

July 1932 and the Prince of Wales is about to inspect the coxswains of Devon's lifeboats. Following is H.M. Smardon, Chairman of Brixham Urban District Council and local Secretary of the RNLI.

Left: *The Prince of Wales and his entourage on the quay inspecting the crew of the Brixham lifeboat.*

Below: *A parade of lifeboatmen led through the town by H.M. Smardon, following the naming of the new lifeboat George Shee, 1932.*

Below left: *Some of the staff at Lupton House, family home of Lord Churston, where the Prince stayed during his visit.*

Quayside scenes at te naming of the George Shee in 1932.

Furzeham football team 1947. Among the names included are Shepherd, Parsons, Mosedale, Coupman, Cold, Fradd and Dunn.

Brixham Wolves FC 1952. Back Row l-r: Mike Harrington, Ken Coram, John Charles, Dave Burrell, Brian Hingston, Ron Bradford, Bill Taylor. Front Row l-r: John Mosedale, John Disney, Ken Crook, Chris Nolan, Brian Muscroft. The club was disbanded in 1955 when the majority of players were called up for National Service.

12 – Sporting Brixham

In this chapter we look at just three of the major sports activities in which Brixham and surrounds has long made a name for itself. The historical aspects only of each is considered for space does not allow coverage of the many hundreds of teams and events that now take place each year.

SOCCER

Perhaps the earliest notice of soccer in Brixham comes from the records of Furzeham Board School which was opened in 1889. Their boys were initiated into the new game by their headmaster Mr W. Bradden. Later there are records from 1904 of a meeting held at Doidge's Temperance Hotel in Fore Street to form a Brixham Association Football Club.

The outbreak of the First World War brought all sporting activities to a standstill and it was not until 1920 that a match was played between Furzeham Rangers (the renamed Brixham United Club) and Brixham Rovers in aid of the Boys' Orphan Home.

By the end of the 1926–7 season Furzeham Rangers were runners up to Paignton Corinthians in the South Devon League. Club players that year included T. Gardiner, F. Gibbs, G. Hatherley, W.E. Weekes, D. Edwards, F. Ward, L. Martin, R. Campion, G. Kennar, A.E. Buley, R. Small, F. Lang, W. Norris, G. Lovegrove, and C. Kent among many others.

At the annual general meeting held in August 1926, Dr R.B. Thompson was elected President, with R.E. Campion Honorary Secretary. A motion by F. Lang that the club's name be changed back to Brixham United was accepted and approved. Later the same season the South Devon Committee invited Brixham United to play in Division 1. By the end of the 1931–2 season the club were runners-up in the First Division, with their home ground in North Fields Lane. A match played in April of that year included L.T. Penwill, W.A. Sanders, L. Martin, F. Lang, S.G. Gibson, A. Worth, S. Clark, D.W. Picek, E.G. Hatherley, R.G. Small and W.G. Norris in the team. By 1936 the club had moved its home ground to Centry Road.

Other clubs formed in the 1930s were Furzeham Rovers and Furzeham Villa, both teams applying to the U.D.C. to play on Furzeham Green. By 1938 Furzeham Rovers were making a name for themselves but with the outbreak of the Second World War once again everything ground to halt. By 1946 Brixham United and Furzeham Villa had managed to restart their club activities and by 1949 could field two teams each, and by the end of that season Brixham United 1st XI had won the Senior Cup in Division 1 of the South Devon League, and the 2nd XI had won the Division 2 Champions Cup.

The two captains at that time were F. Green and W. Edwards and this same season Brixham had produced the first County player from South Devon, S.C. Gibson.

Brixham continues to provide soccer teams providing fierce competition for fellow competitors throughout the region.

Galmpton United 1947-1948. Back Row l-r: *John Crease, Russell Helly, Albert Hoyle, Derek Squires, Stan Usher.* Front Row: *Sammy Dale, Roy Parton, Fred Whitehill, W. Knapman, Tom Cole, Geoff Dunn.*

Eden Park Junior Football Team, 1976. Back Row l-r: Gary Thompson, John Mosedale, Andrew Young, John Holding (Teacher) Bruce Cole, Graham Young, Michael Waiters. Front Row: Andrew Scott, Jonathan King, Philip Ticehurst, Sav Savva (Capt), Wayne Evans, David Bowes, Mark Loram.

The Brixham under 14 Grasshoppers Team which played in the final at Plainmoor against Watcombe Park in 1975. The result after extra time was 1–1 and honours were shared, with each team retaining the cup for six months. Back row l-r: Bill Ivey (Assistant Coach), Steven Ivey, Nick Clyburn, Chris Leaman, Chris Stroud, Billy Williams, Guy Maddocks, Shane Charles, John Charles (Coach). Front Row: David Pillar, Dion Stoyle, Adrian Tribble, Simon Foot, Jimmy Moore, Graham Bardsley.

Brixham RFC 1950-1951. Back Row l-r: *Taff Griffiths, Jim Merchant (Manager - county player 52 times), Brian Lane, Brian Andrews, Wilf Coysh, Fred Charlick, Bob Dart, Albert Hoyle, Maldwyn Jenkins, John Braddick, Bill Dyer.* Front Row: *Bert Caunter, Maurice Andrews, Walter Jackson, Sid Edmonds, Bill Foot, Harold Adams.*

RUGBY

If anything, rugby has an even more illustrious history in Brixham than any other sport. The 'Fishermen' have long been held in high regard and have provided a number of players for the County scene over the years.

CRICKET

The game has been played at Brixham since the late 19th century and a few relics of those early days still survive. For much of period before and after the Second World War the team was captained by Eric Thomas who moved to Brixham

Brixham CC versus International Cricket Crusaders September 1967. Eric Thomas exchanges words with Freddie Truman as he leads out the Brixham team, closely followed by Phil Bond (extreme left Jack Snell (umpire), Geoff Bright (umpire), John Grontenrath, Colin Milburn, Bill Blackler and Jim Parks.

from North Devon. As the club look back on those memorable 'Golden Years' they have much to be proud of. There were no bad teams, it seems, only good teams and better teams. One would like to mention all the players during this time for they all played their part. Nevertheless, the wrath of the hallowed willow would fall upon me were I not to mention names like Eric Thomas, Bill Blackler, Martin Upham, Arthur Crang, Mick Leary and Terry Harper.

In Terry Harper's memoirs he recalls that in August 1945 the team that took the field that day would have been approved by the Church of England being compared with *Ancient and Modern.*

'We travelled to Greenway Ferry,' he said, 'in an old Rolls Royce which had done service during the war as a hearse, pungent with the aromatic scent of embalming fluid and moth balls.'

Selection in those days was not the problem which it has now become. Three people *had* to be selected – they had cars! The umpire and the scorer were automatic choices and the remaining eight were chosen on size – whether they fitted into the available car space! Later selection became more democratic and the team was chosen on merit, unless someone's mother, wife or girl-friend was on teas, then he was sure of a place. Yes, they were great days.

Brixham CC 1st and 2nd XIs, 1975. Back Row l-r: *A. Jarrowson (scorer), D. Hollingworth, T Brookes-Daw, D. Greenaway, P. Preston, T. Billsborough, A. Franklin, N. Harvey, P. Wibrow, J. Pepper, J. Wade, D. Mills (umpire), A. Jago, K. Short, P. Robinson F. Collin, H. Chavasse (umpire), R. Graham, R. Slater.* Front Row: *E. Nolan, G. Breyley, R. How, B. Orchard, M. Freed.*

13 – The *Mayflower* Experience

Among the vast populations of the USA and the United Kingdom there are many who wish to encourage development of relations between the two countries. One such man was Warwick Charlton who decided to turn that wish into reality. The connection, he felt, should be made by a reawakening of the link of ancestry between the two countries through the sailing of the *Mayflower* in 1620 and with the landing of the Pilgrim Fathers in Massachusetts. Could a replica be built and men found willing and brave enough to sail such a frail ship across the wild Atlantic?

The voyage would be made from Plymouth, England, in circumstances as near as possible to those of the first *Mayflower,* and arrive at Plymouth, Massachusetts, within Cape Cod Bay where the Pilgrim Fathers first landed. The north Atlantic is a very large area of water covering some 95 000 square miles with its northern latitude subject to some of the most violent storms of any ocean. The question was how would this replica 17th century galleon fare when at the mercy of the sea. All this was given intensive consideration during the planning and production of the new *Mayflower.*

One of the most important decisions to be made was the complement of a suitable crew, beginning with an experienced sailing captain. With little hesitation, seasoned master mariner Alan Villiers was selected. His experience of sailing windjammers across the oceans of the world made him a popular choice. Later, this experience was to prove invaluable.

Applications for enrolment as crew members were numerous. One was received from Commander Kenelm Winslow, a descendent of Edward Winslow who sailed in the first *Mayflower,* and who was invited to officiate at the formal 'keel-laying' and so provide a connection with the original Pilgrims. Commander Winslow's son John, an expert yachtsman and swimmer, thus became an obvious choice. The crew of *Mayflower II* were as follows:

Commander Alan Villiers D.S.C – Master.
Godfrey Wicksteed – First Mate.

Mayflower II nearing the end of her epic transatlantic voyage in 1957.

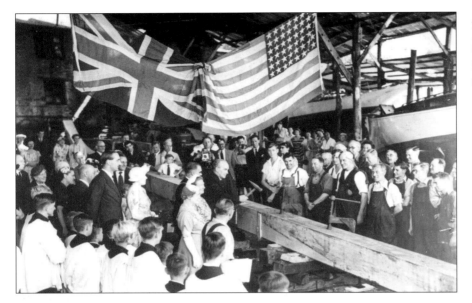

Laying the keel of Mayflower II *at Upham's shipyard, 1956. Commander Winslow wields the hammer while shipwrights and invited guests look on.*

The skills of expert artisans and craftsmen were required if the Mayflower II *were to survive the voyage to America.*

The ribs of the hull nearing completion in 1956.

Left: *Brixham women dressed as Puritans watching the workmen build the hull of* Mayflower II.

Below: *Workers prepare another cross beam for* Mayflower II's *hull, led by head shipwright Jack Buckler who lived to the age of 102 years.*

Inset below: *Ship's carpenter Edgar Mugridge, one of the crew.*

Adrian Small – Second Mate.
Captain Jan Junker – Third Mate.
Stuart Upham – Master Builder
Ike Marsh – Bosun.
Warwick Charlton – instigator and promoter.
Anderson Bell, Dick Brennan, D. Cauvin,
C. Church, F. Edwards, M. Ford, J. Goddard.
W. Goddard (cook), J. Horrocks (radio operator), J. Lacey, A. Lindsay, J. Meany Jr, E. Mugridge (ship's carpenter), G. Nunn, P. Padfield, J. Powell, J. Scarr, H. Sowerby, B. Watson. Dr J. Stevens (surgeon seaman), D.Thorpe, Lt J. Winslow, L. Israel and J. Lugrin, (cameramen), M. Edey and G. Tenney (*Life* Magazine), and 'Felix' the ship's cat.

Warwick Charlton had met Stuart Upham at his shipyard in Brixham and after much discussion a contract was agreed on the 4 July (American Independence Day), 1955. For such a mammoth undertaking only the very best artisans and craftsmen could be employed. Their skills and experience were fundamental to the success of the

enterprise, and indeed to the safety of the ship and all who would sail in her.

The laying of the keel at Upham's shipyard, Brixham, was an impressive affair with the Union flag and the Stars and Stripes poised over a huge block of timber hewn from a 120-year-old oak. The short service was conducted by the Reverend Yeomans followed by Commander Winslow formally tapping the timber keel to complete the ceremony.

Gradually the ship took shape, rising from a raw-boned skeleton to finally emerge as an historically accurate replica of the original *Mayflower*. There had been some earlier misgivings about her sea-worthiness and at her launching on 22 September 1956, as she slid into the water she toppled over to starboard like a drunken sailor. The pessimists had a field-day, giving little hope of the ship ever emulating the achievements of her predecessor. But the unfortunate incident had nothing to do with faults of construction. The problem had been caused by an unusual tide, and once in deep water and correctly ballasted she

The hull and upperworks complete, the builders celebrate their superb task.

Captain Villiers with the Lord Mayor of Plymouth on the Mayflower Steps, 1957.

quickly assumed an even keel. But she was still an unfinished hull and a lot of work had to be done before completion.

Present at the launch was the Chairman of the Brixham Urban District Council, Councillor Fred Buley, and Mrs Ella Buley, Warwick Charlton, Stuart Upham, many shipyard employees and invited guests.

On the evening of the 17 April 1957, the little ship set out from Brixham and, because of the adverse wind, was towed around Scabbacombe Head and the Mew Stone to Dartmouth, and from thence to Plymouth Sound. A call at both ports was necessary for the original *Mayflower* had done this in 1620. An especially colourful ceremony greeted her at Plymouth's Mayflower Steps on the Barbican Quay from which the Pilgrim Fathers had originally boarded their little barque. The Lord Mayor of Plymouth, England, the Chairman of the Board of Selectmen of Plymouth, Massachusetts, and many dignitaries in their red robes, were there. Captain Villiers arrived in a long boat, dressed in his best Pilgrim suit, his crew regaled in similar costumes.

The vessel set out from Plymouth on 20 April hoping for a strong easterly wind. Instead, the sea was flat calm and the becalmed *Mayflower II* had to accept a tow to clear the land and to pick up the Channel winds.

It took two days before *Mayflower II* reached the sail-filling winds of the Atlantic. The first few days were quiet but on the fourth day the sky assumed a vague menacing luminosity and the sea began to build up with serried waves of green-grey marching uniformly along, topped with frothing caps of white. Soon long ribbons streaked the water as wave troughs began to deepen, their tops blown off and carried as spume. But the *Mayflower* had been built by men of the sea, masters of their trade, and each with a lifetime of experience, and she withstood all that the storm could throw at her.

As the voyagers neared Bermuda, steamers and liners, tankers and traders slowed in welcome salute and later, American and British destroyers formed an unofficial escort. But the highlight came when the great British aircraft-carrier *Ark Royal* slowed to their own speed and escorted her.

Thus for a moment on the bridge of time, the past and present, the old and the new, each in courteous recognition of the other paused, the one acknowledging the courageous endeavours of a past age.

Old World meets New World. Aircraft Carrier Ark Royal *escorts* Mayflower II *as she nears the end of her transatlantic voyage.*

Dressed in their smart sailor suits, boys of the British Seaman's Orphan Boy's Home march to Sunday parade, February 1936.

A view of the Orphanage from the seaward side, c.1920.

Entitled 'A late volunteer for the Sailor's Hornpipe', this cartoon was presented to the author's father in 1914 by the famous cartoonist Alfred Leese.

14 – The Call of the Sea

THE BRITISH SEAMEN'S ORPHAN BOY'S HOME

In 1861, a William Gibbs of Clyst St George, near Exeter, took a house in Brixham for the care of the sons of deceased seamen. Two years later he had a new building erected nearby where 10 boys could be admitted. By 1873, an extension to the premises allowed accommodation for 50 boys, and by 1906 this had risen to 60 boys. The marble memorial on the 'South Wall' to three of the staff and fourteen boys killed in the 1914–1918 war was carved by Messrs Shrives of Brixham.

Over the years, the Boy's Home had been supported by voluntary contributions, but in September 1937 it was agreed that the Home should be discontinued as a school, with the boys in future attending the National School and with eligibility to attend Torquay Grammar School.

THE SEA CADETS

The Brixham Sea Cadet movement was established during the Second World War, in 1943, and in the absence of suitable permanent, headquarters the Admiralty provided a Motor Torpedo Boat (MTB 609) for their activities, with Chief Petty Officer Instructor Alan Widdicombe (later Lieutenant Widdicombe) as trainer and teacher, and with Admiral Turnbull as Chairman of the Committee. Eventually, the Sea Cadet Council of the Navy League offered, free of charge, a Nissen hut, and in November 1948 the new headquarters was ready at Mount Pleasant quarry. The opening ceremony was performed by Captain Hugh Faulkner (later Admiral Faulkner), Captain of Dartmouth Royal Naval College, with Mrs Faulkner declaring their new home as 'Training ship HMS *Brixham*'.

Captain Faulkner's name has an important place in Second World War naval history. In May 1942, he was captain of the heavy cruiser HMS *Edinburgh*. The ship left Murmansk carrying £45 million worth of the former Czar of Russia's gold bullion, payment for the thousands of tanks, guns and aircraft supplied by the Allies to the Russians in their efforts to defeat Hitler's armies on the Eastern front.

Prior to a march through the town the band of the Seaman's Orphan Boy's Home proudly present their musical instruments.

On the ship's return voyage to England, *Edinburgh* was hit by torpedoes. Sinking and helpless in the water, she was attacked by three German destroyers, but in her dying moments her remaining gun destroyed the leading enemy ship and the raid was abandoned. However, despite gallant attempts to save her, *Edinburgh* sank below the icy Arctic waters with the gold still aboard.

Exactly forty years later, a salvage company pinpointed the wreck and recovered all the bullion. Of the 700 men on the ship 68 were killed but it was only by the skill and fine leadership of Captain Hugh Faulkner that the loss of life was not greater.

Ironically, some years after the end of the war while on his farm in Somerset, the tractor he was driving rolled over and killed him. It was indeed a tragic end to a life filled with narrow escapes and adventure.

57 Unit Sea Cadet Corps (Brixham), 1948. First row l-r: *Williams, Lovegrove, Perrett, Lane, Taylor, Mumery, York, Mathay, Johnson, Worth.* Second row: *Thompson, Gregory, Stevens, Hoskins, Cumming, Oram, Jordain.* Third row: *Warren, Harding, Holloway, Lee, Widdicombe, Jones, Holloway, Burley, Passmore, Rockey, Fradd.* Fourth row: *Caper, Shears, Williams, Dalley, Guy, Coysh, ? , Milton.*

15 – Scenes Between the Wars

The 1920s saw great social upheaval in the country. Men returning from the horrors of the First World War found themselves out of work and with their dreams of a better future turned to dust. Poverty and hunger were common.

In contrast the 1930s, known to some as the 'lost decade' brought some improvement and hope although the Depression of the early thirties brought unemployment and misery to many. Britain's once great Empire was fragmenting and the Establishment increasingly came under question. Despite the threat of conflict in Europe due to the rise of National Socialism in Germany, the ordinary men and women of Britain were beginning to find a new sense of independence from the old order.

Brixham, though maintaining much of its tradition was also facing change. The photos included here bring back some of the sights and scenes in the area during this period of great transition.

The foundation of the Breakwater was laid in 1843 and eventually stretched 1400 feet out into the bay. Over the years extensions have been made until, on completion in 1916, its length totalled 3000 feet, with the total cost amounting in excess of £100 000.

In the past vast quantities of limestone were quarried at sites around Brixham, especially at Berry Head, Freshwater and Breakwater quarries. The industry of lime-burning had long died out but traces of the old kilns remain.

BRIXHAM. FRESHWATER FROM OVERGANG

The steep ascent of the 44 Bay View Steps, c.1920.

Three of the officials of the 1920 Brixham regatta stand at their posts on the regatta boat. Left to right: H.M. Smardon, Sir Alfred Goodson and Tom Lovell.

Officials of the Torbay lifeboat at Brixham, 1927. Left to right marked x: H. Slade (Secretary), W. Sanders (Coxswain), J. Gill (District Officer Coastguards), H.M. Smardon (Secretary Kingswear, Brixham and Torbay).

Top: *The lower end of Fore Street in the 1890s. Stone's general store stood here on the 'Island' until its demolition in 1908 when it was replaced by Lloyds Bank* (lower picture) *at the corner of Pump Street.*

Janes' Corner Dairy at King Street decorated with flags to celebrate Empire Day in 1932. The Morris 8 van, registration number ETA 211 advertises cream by post - note the van's twin sister has the number ETA 210.

The old Cottage Hospital in Cavern Road, Brixham, was opened in 1895 at a cost of £1500, a sum funded by a Miss A.M. Hogg. The work in the hospital was carried out under her personal supervision through a hospital committee. A number of fishermen formed themselves into a band of workmen and were known as the 'Brothers of Pity'.

Fishing boats at rest in the harbour, 1920.

This photograph was taken in 1937 at the time of the Coronation of King George VI. The man in the yachting cap is H.M. Smardon, Secretary of the Regatta Committee for over 50 years, secretary of many other committees and Chairman of Brixham Urban District Council. He also taught at Furzeham School where one of his pupils was James Callaghan who, in 1964, was to become Chancellor of the Exchequer and later Foreign Secretary. The headmaster at Furzeham at that time was Mr Fred Pady. The picture line-up of Council Officers is (left to right): C. Johns (Water Bailiff), C. Edwards (Councillor), S. Lear (Town Clerk), Councillors W. Smardon, J. Owen, H. Smardon, F. Lee, L.J. Boyce and H. Silley.

Above: *The interior of All Saints Church, Brixham.*

Right: *St Mary's Church dates from 1425.*

Below: *The interior of St Peter's Church, Brixham.*

16 – The Second World War

While Hitler's rise to power went unchecked in Europe, Britain was slow to prepare herself for what was to be a second world conflict. However, the military were not entirely oblivious to the threat of war and the area around Brixham was once again preparing itself for the fight.

The defensive role of the guns at Battery Gardens was to thwart attacks by sea and to serve as an anti-aircraft station. The site at Brixham Battery, and a similar at Corbyn's Head, Torquay, were two of many sited along the south coast. Their function was to defend the local beaches against enemy landings such as those at Torre Abbey, Livermead, Hollicombe, Preston, Paignton, Goodrington, Broadsands and Elbury Cove.

In 1940 the site was manned initially by the Royal Artillery but later by units of the Home Guard on a part time basis by local men. Despite their non-professionalism the crews became very efficient and were often commended by the Brigadier Southern Command. There were many occasions on which the AA defence guns at the Battery were in action against the hit-and-run raiders attacking Brixham harbour and shipping in the Bay. These included Messerschmitt 109s carrying 500lb bombs and later the Focke-Wulf 190s with formidable 1000lb bomb loads. The Battery Observation post was situated at the highest elevation where it could command the best view, while the Bofors anti-aircraft gun and rocket projector were sited on gently sloping land behind and away from the main guns. At several other places in the grounds were other guns, searchlight emplacements and Nissen huts.

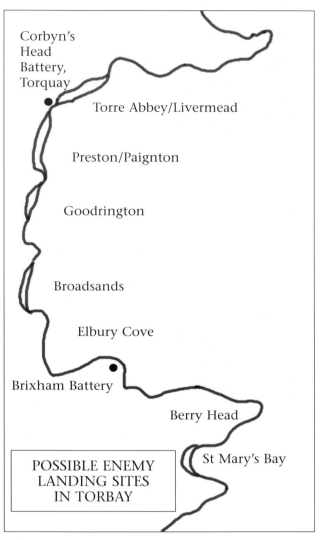

Corbyn's Head Battery, Torquay

Torre Abbey/Livermead

Preston/Paignton

Goodrington

Broadsands

Elbury Cove

Brixham Battery

Berry Head

St Mary's Bay

POSSIBLE ENEMY LANDING SITES IN TORBAY

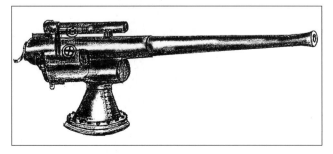

Coastal battery 4.7-inch gun as installed at Brixham.

Practice shoots took place once every two months during the evenings and also at night for the benefit of the searchlight crews. Targets would be towed across the bay by a motor launch and comprised a pair of frames about 10 feet long and 6 feet high, these frames being 100 yards apart and connected to the towing launch by a long tow line. The distance between the frames was intended to represent the bow-to-stern location of an enemy vessel.

On the main road at the entrance to Battery Gardens is a patch of grass near a seat. This was the site of the Bofor's anti-aircraft gun which during the war was used frequently against hit-and-run raiders.

Practice shooting at a drogue towed past the battery by a friendly aircraft was not the most popular occupation of our RAF pilots. On one such occasion a shell actually exploded in front of the aircraft. The very frightened pilot frantically signalled to the gun crew 'I am pulling this bloody thing, not pushing it!'

Today Battery Gardens provide a pleasant environment for both locals and visitors alike, and the remains of the fortifications do not intrude upon the surroundings, a tribute to the efficient care of the local council. The Gardens also stand as a memorial to those who served there and to those who lived close to the gun sites.

DUNKIRK AND AFTER

When the German dictator Adolf Hitler 'let loose the dogs of war' in 1939, Britain found herself defenceless, naked and vulnerable, facing the impossible task of trying to repair the damage caused by the negligence of its leaders of the time. With the advance of German tanks and troops across France, driving the British army back towards the Channel ports, the Government issued urgent appeals for boats, large and small, to sail to Dunkirk to rescue as many men as possible.

Several Brixham boats were out fishing when the call came, but those men still ashore hastily collected drums of fuel while womenfolk prepared food.

The first boat to leave Brixham was a pleasure vessel with Skipper E. Harris and T. Bowes aboard. The next day two convoys of small boats set off manned by men between the ages of 50 and 70 years. In total, from all parts of the Channel coast, 861 vessels arrived at Dunkirk to accomplish the greatest rescue in British history. Over 338,000 men were plucked to safety. After the fall of France the invasion of Britain seemed inevitable. In South Devon inshore boat patrols, armed only with rifles and Very pistols, sailed from Brixham, Dartmouth, Teignmouth and Salcombe, providing a nightly patrol of six boats comprising yachts, small craft and some Brixham and Belgian trawlers

Later, the Admiralty requisitioned the quays and wharfs around Brixham harbour including Upham's shipyard and the premises of Torbay Trawlers Ltd. Brixham was considered an ideal port with its docking and building facilities and this was evidenced by the construction or repair of over 1000 small naval vessels during the war.

The Northcliffe Hotel was also requisitioned for marine personnel including three Admiralty representatives.

Although a large part of her army had been

A parade of an early Brixham Home Guard unit, 1940.

A unit of Brixham's Home Guard march through the streets led by the Commanding Officer Lt-Col. W. Parsons in 1940. Note the Triumph motorcycle - a popular means of transport when petrol rationing was introduced.

saved, Britain now stood alone facing the threat of invasion and it was at this time that Winston Churchill, with his indomitable spirit, proclaimed 'We shall defend our island whatever the cost. We shall never surrender'.

However, he was careful to add that although the Dunkirk operation could be considered a victory 'Wars are not won by evacuations'. Britain now had to take the offensive and an appeal was made for men who had not yet been called-up to come forward to create a Home Guard contingent.

At Brixham 119 volunteers reported for duty to form the first Group which was then divided into three sections under the command of Captain Hay-Matthey of Laywell House. This included men from Higher Brixham, Lower Brixham, Kingswear, Churston and Galmpton. Unfortunately the only weapons available were six double-barrel shotguns used for shooting rabbits, a few .22 sporting rifles and six truncheons!

Suitable accommodation for the Home Guard Headquarters was also a constant problem. The first section made theirs at the old hospital in Cavern Hill, the second in a cowshed at Ranscombe, and a third at Galmpton Warborough public lavatories.

On one occasion, when the entire local Home Guard was assembled for inspection, Captain Matthey approached an elderly corporal:

'Now my man, what would you do if you were suddenly confronted by an armed Nazi storm trooper?'

'Oh, I'd shoot the b—,' said Thompson.

Captain Matthey was shocked 'No, no,no,' said he, 'You would capture him.'

'Not bloody likely,' declared Thompson, 'I'd shoot 'un.'

It seems that the Corporal had his own rules on how the war should be conducted .

In 1940 Lt-Col. W. Parsons assumed command of the company, responsible for the defence of twelve miles of coastline from Broadsands to Kingswear. By this time, 4-inch and 4.7-inch guns had been installed at Corbyn's Head Torquay, at

Members of a Brixham Home Guard unit pose for their photograph, 1940.

Battery Gardens, Brixham, and at Brownstone, Kingswear. Some of this ordnance carried worn brass plates on the muzzle marked 'Japan 1902'. These were examples of the weapons with which Britain was expected to defend herself!

In the early weeks of the war at sea Britain suffered many reverses, resulting in casualties and tragedies affecting a number of families in Brixham.

BRIXHAM HONOURS AND DECORATIONS

During the Second World War many decorations and honours were awarded to Brixham men, a number of them from the navy, four of which are included here.

Shipwright W.J. Shears of 'Sunnydale', Burton Street, was the first Brixham man to be killed on active service. He was one of the 500 who lost their lives when the aircraft carrier HMS *Courageous* was torpedoed by a German U-boat on the 17 September, 1939, in the north Atlantic, west of Ireland.

Chief Engine Room Artificer Frederick Ward of the Buller's Arms on the Strand, was Mentioned in Despatches while serving in the ill-fated battleship HMS *Prince of Wales* when she and HMS *Repulse* were sunk by Japanese bombers north of Singapore in December 1941. Two Brixham men saved from HMS *Repulse* were S.H. Hall of New Road and First Class Boy A.J. Weekes of South Furzeham Road.

Lieutenant Stafford Hook of Summer Lane was Mentioned in Dispatches on the 14 January 1941 for his courage, enterprise and devotion to duty whilst serving in the Aircraft Carrier HMS *Eagle* while under aerial attack outside Tobruk.

Chief Petty Officer George Mills originally of 12 Trafalgar Square, Higher Furzeham Road, was awarded the DSM for courage and outstanding skill in the cruiser HMS *Exeter* in the naval battle with the German pocket battleship *Graf Spee* in December 1939.

HMS BRIXHAM

HMS *Brixham* was part of the Royal Navy's Minesweeping Flotilla serving in the Mediterranean in the Second World War. In 1942 she escorted the invasion force during Operation Torch, the invasion of North Africa, and later maintained her sweeping role along the South African coast. She also took part in the perilous action at the invasion of Sicily (Operation Husky in 1943), and was subjected to heavy bombing attacks in both these campaigns. Later HMS *Brixham* was employed in clearing coastal waters prior to the Anzio beach landings and went on to continue her service in the Med until the end of the war.

Devon people hold a great affection for the ships which carried the name of their towns and no doubt the people of Brixham felt a pride in the vital part their namesake warship played.

HMS Brixham.

Minesweeping was one of the most dangerous operations to be undertaken by the Royal Navy. and these little ships had to venture into mine-infested waters to clear channels through which British ships could pass.

Many minesweepers were blown up and hundreds of lives lost but the operations had to go on, regardless. HMS *Brixham* was indeed fortunate to have survived these major campaigns in which courage and resolve played no small part. Her memory will live on.

HOME FRONT

During the bombing raids on Torbay in 1942, Sgt W.P. Meadows, a Brixham man, was the first member of a Home Guard unit in the South West to bring down an enemy aircraft. When three German FW190s attacked Hollicombe Gas Works, Sgt Meadows discharged ten rounds of rocket projectiles and destroyed the leading bomber.

The ladies of Brixham played their part too. Here in 1940 the photograph overleaf shows the lady members of the British Legion knitting circle who are busy producing scarves and socks for the fighting men. These garments were particularly appreciated by those who served in the Arctic on the dreaded Russian convoys.

WARTIME RATIONING.

The gravest point of the war was in 1941–1942 when German submarines were sinking thousands of tons of our food imports in the Battle of the Atlantic. Rationing was the only answer.

Even in 1940 housewives in Brixham, as indeed elsewhere, learned that restrictions would apply to such things as butter, sugar, tea, bacon, meat etc. and one person's ration for a week amounted to: tea – 2 oz, sugar – 8 oz, butter – 2 oz, bacon – 4 oz, cheese – 1 oz, and so on. The butcher's reply to any grumbles was usually 'Haven't you heard

Focke Wulf 190 of the type that made many hit-and-run raids on Torbay.

The Brixham British Legion knitting circle, 1940.

"DRIED EGGS are my eggs — my whole eggs and nothing but my eggs"

Dried eggs are the complete hen's eggs, both the white and the yolk, dried to a powder. Nothing is added. Nothing but moisture and the shell taken away, leaving the eggs themselves as wholesome, as digestible and as full of nourishment and health-protecting value as if you had just taken the eggs new laid from the nest. So put the eggs back into your breakfast menus. And what about a big, creamy omelette for supper? You can have it savoury; or sweet, now that you get extra jam.

DRIED EGGS build you up!

In war-time, the most difficult foods for us to get are the body-builders. Dried eggs build muscle and repair tissue in just the same way as do chops and steaks; and are better for health-protection. So we are particularly lucky to be able to get dried eggs to make up for any shortage of other body-builders such as meat, fish, cheese, milk.

Your allowance of DRIED EGG is equal to 3 eggs a week

You can now get one 12-egg packet (price 1 3 per 4-week rationing period — three fine fresh eggs a week, at the astonishingly low price of 1½d. each. Children (holders of green ration books) get two packets each rationing period. You buy your dried eggs at the shop where you are registered for shell eggs; poultry keepers can buy any where.

Don't hoard your dried eggs; use them up — there are plenty more coming!

Note. *Don't make up dried eggs until you are ready to use them; they should not be allowed to stand after they've been mixed with water or other liquid. Use dry when making cakes and so on, and add a little more moisture when mixing.*

FREE — DRIED EGG LEAFLET containing many interesting recipes, will be sent on receipt of a postcard addressed to Dept. 627E, Food Advice Service, Ministry of Food, London, W.1.

ISSUED BY THE MINISTRY OF FOOD

Fruitful results from vegetables

Eating fruit is a pleasure we don't often get nowadays, and there's no denying we miss it. But, from the point of view of health, we can more than make up for the lack of fruit by eating extra vegetables.

The main health value of fruit is in its Vitamin C. Vitamin C clears the skin, prevents fatigue, and helps you to resist infection. And it's by no means confined to oranges, as people are apt to imagine. Some vegetables, indeed, actually contain *more* of this health-giver than oranges do.

get your requirement of amin C you should eat ly a salad which includes od portion of at least one ie following:

atercress (all the year round)
w shredded sprouts (December to February)
w shredded cabbage (May o August, October to March)
w shredded spinach (all ie year round)
edded swede or turnip ieptember to March)
Vitamin C value will be eased if you use parsley mustard and cress as a iish.

used servings of ked green vegetables ced swedes and turnips ced potatoes iiso help to maintain the iin C value of the diet at h level.

bles are most "fruitful" nin C when you serve w !

y the way, the dark eaves of vegetables her in vitamins and than the paler insides. n they're too tough iw, or to cook in the way, be sure to put o soups or stews.

friend the carrot, not so rich in C, is t for its anti-infective i.

Have YOU tried DRIED EGGS yet?

Dried Egg from America is now in the shops — soon there'll be enough for one 1/9d. tin on every ration book ... they are extra to your regular egg ration. Each tin contains one dozen fine fresh eggs, dried, and in powder form. Nothing is taken away but the shells and water. All the rich goodness and fine flavour of fresh egg remain.

You get your Dried Eggs from where you are registered for shell eggs. Mix with water as directed on the tin and use just as you would use freshly beaten egg.

...ED BY THE MINISTRY OF FOOD

Contemporary advice from the Ministry of Food c.1943.

there's a war on?' People 'made do' with less food and with little new clothing. Surprisingly, the general health of the nation improved, or so it was claimed. Clothing and stockings became early victims, relegated to a points system with a yearly allowance rationed to 66 points.

THE YANKS ARE COMING

Following Japan's bombing and destruction of the American fleet at Pearl Harbor in December 1941, Britain gained the support of a great ally which made not only the defeat of Nazi Germany possible but brought millions of US soldiers to this country in preparation for the invasion of Europe.

In the autumn of 1943, the Royal Naval College at Dartmouth was taken over by the US Naval Task Force and training began for the invasion of France with the entire area between Slapton and Blackawton taken over as a live-ammunition battle area for the training of the invasion forces.

The code name for the invasion was 'Overlord', and in the final weeks before D-Day, there was a whole series of heart-stopping incidents, each of which could have leaked the secret to the waiting enemy. In Exeter a railway employee found a briefcase abandoned in a train compartment. In it was a complete set of Overlord plans.

On a morning in Whitehall, four weeks before the invasion, a gust of wind blew a dozen copies of the Overlord plan into the street. Security officers raced out and chased papers amongst the traffic. They only recovered eleven copies but after two hours, the twelfth copy was handed in by an unknown civilian. Security was so vital to the success of the operation that idle chit-chat was a constant threat.

New routes into Brixham were planned in readiness for D-Day and, to facilitate the passage of tanks, several shops and houses were demolished and roads widened, with hards and piers constructed for the berthing of LSTs (Landing Ship Tanks) and LCIs (Landing Craft Infantry).

In the midst of the battle exercises a terrible tragedy occurred in Lyme Bay on the night of 27 May 1944 during a final seaborne rehearsal in which over 300 ships took part. The convoy was suddenly attacked by a fleet of German E-boats off Portland resulting in the death of 700 US troops.

At Brixham, Salcombe and Dartmouth and many other ports along the South coast of England, a total of 7000 seacraft were waiting

Us troops on parade in Brixham in 1943, seen here passing the Town Hall.

United States General Eisenhower, Supreme Commander of Allied Invasion Forces, British Prime Minister Winston Churchill, and US General Bradley do a little target practice when on a tour of inspection at Slapton Sands. Eisenhower and Bradley scored hits but Winston's target was tactfully removed before his score could be counted.

These two views show the action on the beaches of Slapton as US troops train for the invasion of D-Day. A large area of the South Hams was evacuated and closed to all but military personnel. Despite the massive movements of troops their ultimate destination, the beaches of Normandy, and the date of the invasion was kept entirely secret from the enemy.

Motor Torpedo Boats moored alongside Brixham breakwater 1944. These little craft performed sterling service in the fight against the enemy throughout the war. The MTBs carried two 21-inch torpedoes, rapid firing guns and a crew of ten. Capable of 48 knots, or 54 mph, their mission was to attack enemy shipping along the coast of occupied France.

US troops aboard their LCTs are ready for the invasion of Normandy. Many Americans would lose their lives in the first waves ashore on the fateful morning of 6 June 1944.

loaded with 200 000 assault troops packed into landing barges, ready to go. In support there were 11 000 paratroopers and thousands of gliders. During the last days and nights of May, army tanks and military vehicles rumbled and clattered their way towards embarkation points, joined by the tramp, tramp, tramp of army boots.

On the 6 June 1944, Operation Overlord, the invasion of Normandy, began with a massive assault on German strongholds and forts, the culmination of months of training in Devon.

The Allied advance continued until 7 May 1945, when all German Forces surrendered unconditionally. The 8 May was celebrated as VE Day (Victory in Europe). Three months later, on 14 August 1945, following the dropping of two atom bombs on Japanese cities, Japan surrendered to American forces, with 15 August acknowledged as VJ Day (Victory in Japan).

The Second World War was over and with it came peace at last, but at what a price! It had lasted five years, cost the lives of 60 million people

US troops and equipment are gathered for embarkation at Brixham hard June 1944, en route to Utah Beach, Normandy.

A scene on the Normandy beachhead in the days following the successful invasion of France in June 1944. Much of the success was the result of arduous training in South Devon.

and brought tragedy and misery to hundreds of millions of others.

Peace also brought the disbanding of many service units and the diffraction of large bodies of people who had been bound together by a common adversity. But in the meantime, VE Day and VJ Day meant celebrations and many a street party was held in towns throughout Britain to mark the occasions, not least in Brixham and Churston Ferrers where people pooled what few rations they had to create a memorable treat for the children.

Victory in Europe was greeted with joy and celebration. There was sadness too as the toll of war became apparent. Once the euphoria had died down there were new problems to be faced as couples sought desperately to find a place of their own.

One local child has vivid memories of the day: 'As children on VE Day, we stood to attention in the school playground to sing the National Anthem, 'Land of Hope and Glory', and 'Jerusalem'. Hundreds of union jacks and streamers fluttered in the breeze as we had street parties to celebrate the homecoming of sailors and soldiers. For the children it was a wonderful time.'

For a few weeks people were able to forget the continuing problems and uncertainties that had filled their lives for five years. Despite food rationing and fears for those who had still not returned from war, the nation set about organising celebrations and memorial services with great enthusiasm.

Once again the people of the country were joined in patriotic fervour, a sense of achievement in overcoming a wicked power in Europe, and a pride in what Britain and her allies had achieved. In Brixham the events leading up to D Day had brought its people close to the front line and the photographs on the following pages reflect the sense of fun and enjoyment these celebrations brought to the town.

Just about the whole village of Churston Ferrers turned out for the VE Day celebration. Among those present are Mr and Mrs Hugh Goodson, Mrs Fox and Jim Fox, Mrs Raby, Mr and Mrs Winsor, Mr and Mrs Wakeham, Maurice Wakeham and Miss Wakeham, Mrs Damerel, Mr and Mrs Gagg and Norman Gagg, Rose Baker, Mr and Mrs Rundle, Mrs Preston, Jean Preston and Miss Preston, Mrs Weekes, Mary Gagg, Mary Bond, Mary Jury, Wendy McCarthy, Mr and Mrs Ley, Mrs Carlo and curate Rev. Bonsey.

Another great day for the children of Churston Ferrers to remember. VJ Day, the end of the war with Japan, is celebrated in August 1945. Among those present are Doris Gagg, Mary Bond, Jean Preston, Maurice Wakeham, Ken Jury, Mary Jury, Mary Gagg, Billy Wakeham, Stella Maunder, David Maunder, Richard Bawden, Billy Maunder, Wendy McCarthy and curate Rev. Bonsey.

Children of Higher Street celebrate VE Day at a typical street party, August 1945.

The vogue for street parties continued throughout the decade and these children are celebrating the Coronation of Elizabeth II in 1952. Sweet rationing had only just ended!

THE REFUGEES RETURN

When in 1940 German troops swept through the low countries, many Belgians endeavoured to escape. Belgian fishermen who already knew Brixham, arrived with only what they stood up in. Once again Brixham rose to the occasion and offered help, food and accommodation, and by 1941, the Belgian community which had settled into Brixham life numbered around 2000. On 21 November, 1941, on the celebration of the opening of the new Belgian Club, a Belgian flag flew over Brixham Town Hall. By 1942 there were 95 Belgian trawlers fishing out of the port

However in the weeks leading up to D Day these trawlers had to leave Brixham temporarily

Brixham men return home from their service units following demobilisation in 1945.

Belgian refugees played a considerable role in Brixham's wartime years. They had arrived in their fishing boats in 1939 following the German invasion of Belgium, bringing with them much of their furniture and effects. Welcomed by the people of Brixham they stayed on until the end of the war, continuing their fishing, and leaving much as they had arrived, the decks of their vessels piled high with their worldly goods.

to allow the invasion force freedom of movement. They soon returned once the Normandy landings had been completed.

After VE Day 1945, Belgian families started to return to their own country resulting in many sad farewells. On 17 August Brixham folk gathered at the quayside to bid 'bon voyage' as twenty Belgian trawlers bedecked with flags, headed out to sea. The last to leave was the *Pierre* (0281), formerly the Brixham smack *Superb* (BM1) stacked with furniture lashed to the deck. In 1946 when Councillor C.M. Ashford, former Chairman of the Brixham U.D.C. visited Heist in Belgium in 1946,

he was overwhelmed with the welcome he received and the gift of a model of a Brixham trawler in brass on a marble base.

Around this time an event worth recording was the appearance in Brixham harbour of Commander A.R. Alston OBE, Commanding Officer, HMS *Vernon*, Teignmouth. He and his crew, gave a demonstration to show the work of frogmen as human minesweepers. To the many residents and visitors it was their first sight of a diver dressed in a rubber suit and helmet, with flippers on his feet. The demonstration was in aid of King George's Fund for Sailors and raised £400.

Brixham Town Hall 1942. As a token of Goodwill the retired fishermen of Brixham received gift parcels from the people of South Africa, distributed by the mayor (centre front).

Remembrance Day, 11 November 1946. Wreath laying at the war memorial in Berry Head Road in remembrance of those who died in two world wars.

Left and below: *In the years immediately following the war life was still austere, rationing continued and employment was difficult to come by. However, perhaps because of this, communities were anxious to celebrate whenever an opportunity presented itself. The surroundings may be less than salubrious but the Youth Club Annual Social Supper, held in the Town Hall in December 1946, attracted a large and enthusiastic gathering.*

A shopper in Fox Lane, in the 1940s. Rationing and general food shortages brought about a thriftiness and a willingness to 'make do and mend' that survived in people long after the war's end. This is in stark contrast to today's consumer society where much of what is purchased is discarded without a second thought.

17 – Floods

The Brixham floods of 1946–47 followed a severe winter. The late thaw and heavy rain at the beginning of March caused the worst flooding in living memory in Brixham. Water from the surrounding hills poured into the town turning the streets into rivers. Union Lane was flooded to a depth of six feet and the only means of escape for people trapped in upper rooms was by means of rowing boats brought in from the quay.

So bad were the conditions that a ferry boat service was established to bring people from one side of the town to the other. Many were made homeless and they were taken at first to the Methodist Church and later to the British Legion in King Street to be cared for by Mrs Stapleton and her team of helpers. The Iron Foundry furnace in Union Lane was flooded, electric motors damaged and valuable goods swept away. Bolton Cross became a lake extending from the foot of Parkham Hill up Bolton Street and New Road, causing traffic chaos. As a result, buses proceeded no further than Monks Bridge and cars had to be abandoned. For several days there were no signs of the flood subsiding but when it did, a mammoth problem developed in having to clear mud and debris. Some cellars and basements remained flooded for many days. Woolworth's basement store had valuable stock floating around, and in Goad's print room £500 of paper stock was ruined, while in the Electric Cinema in Fore Street 300 seats had to be taken away and thoroughly dried and cleaned.

It was indeed an unforgettable and distressing period in the Town's history.

The great flood of 1947 caused enormous damage in and around Brixham's town centre. The rainstorm produced rivers of water from the steep hillsides around which poured into shops and private dwellings causing losses of thousands of pounds. This photograph of Bolton Cross indicates the height of the water.

A car is trapped in the floodwaters at Bolton Cross.

Below: *A policeman rescues residents in a rowing boat, while two women are brought to safety in Union Lane.*

A bus and a van negotiate the floods in Bolton Street.

18 – Joining Forces

The suggestion that Torquay, Paignton and Brixham should be amalgamated as a county borough was first mooted in 1921 by the Town Clerk of Torquay H.A. Hield. At that time the combined population of the three towns was large enough to constitute a claim to county borough status. Although Brixham was well disposed, the idea did not find acceptance in Paignton and after some discussion the matter was dropped.

On 7th March 1930, the question was again raised in the Brixham Chamber of Trade and Commerce when Richard Couch Elliott urged that the Chamber should do all within its power to influence Paignton to take a more favourable view of the matter. As a result the following resolution was passed on the proposition of H.M. Smardon: 'That the Brixham Chamber of Trade satisfactorily favour the amalgamation of Brixham, Paignton and Torquay and will do their utmost to further

its accomplishment.' No further action was taken until towards the end of 1949 when the Mayor of Torquay also invited the Urban District Councils of Churston and Kingswear to meet to discuss the future with a view to securing the most efficient unit of local government. Paignton again declined stating 'no useful purpose would be served.'

The General Election of February 1950, caused a great many other matters to be discussed, but Brixham Chamber of Trade was still anxious to do all possible to bring about amalgamation with its two neighbours.

In the years that followed, there were many meetings, many resolutions and many amendments to resolutions, but not until 1968 was a decision reached whereby the three towns of Torquay, Paignton and Brixham were finally amalgamated to form the Torbay District Council.

The opening of the new pre-fab houses in Centry Road Brixham in 1948. Those present are l-r: D. Godfrey (Sanitary Engineer), R Mitchell (Treasurer), D. Lenin (Councillor), Mrs Parks (Councillor), P. Thompson (Surveyor), A. Heron (Councillor), C. Ashford (Councillor), H. Smardon (Chairman), R. Braddock (Councillor). Inset: *Brixham's Civic Crest.*

Isabelle Barker in the presence of Brixham Councillors performs the ceremony at the opening of Astley Park gates, installed in memory of her father, Henry Maddock Smardon, Chairman of Brixham UDC for many years. Present l-r: Cllr Ashford, unknown, Mrs Parks (Chairman), Cllr Burgoyne and Mrs Smardon.

Isabelle Barker (née Smardon) touches the tablet to the memory of her late father H.M. Smardon, Chairman of the Council and a leading light in the life of Brixham, 1950.

19 – Happy Campers

Torbay's growth as a holiday resort stemmed from the arrival of the railway. This meant that people who had hitherto no means of transport could travel with ease and comfort to the West Country. Torquay had long been a favourite resort for the wealthy who, in the early Victorian period, had begun to build huge villas overlooking the sea. They came for the bathing, sailing, and for the air – but also simply because it was fashionable. The harbour was filled with expensive yachts.

After the First World War the working classes also found the seaside air to their liking and they flocked in their thousands each summer to spend a few days soaking up the sun. They often stayed in boarding houses or small hotels but as Torbay increased in popularity camping sites provided cheap and plentiful accommodation. Though Torquay and Paignton were favoured destinations, Brixham too found itself the centre of attraction each year as the trains arrived from the Midland towns packed with excited families.

Left: One of the most memorable train journeys in Britain takes the summer visitor along the South Devon coast, through one holiday resort after another: Dawlish, Teignmouth (and changing at Newton Abbot) to Torquay, Paignton and Brixham (via Churston station).

Below: The princess of South Devon resorts, Torquay, once drew a wealthier clientelle than its neighbours.

Magnificent views and seaside air brought tourists in their thousands each year. Berry Head became a favoured destination for a bracing walk.

On a warm sunny day Breakwater Beach provides healthy fun for holidaymakers in the 1950s.

Left: The tennis courts at Dolphin Holiday Camp, 1954.

Below: *A postcard reveals the delights of St Mary's Bay Holiday Camp, 1958. It boasts lawns, chalets, gardens and a communal dining hall.*

Below: *Louville Camp at Paignton is filled with tents, chalets and caravans in 1938. Such camps were forerunners of the famous holiday camps run by Butlins, among others, to provide affordable holidays for the working classes.*

Old Brixham

Bolton Cross, 1895. This, and the view below reminds us of the timeless tranquillity of life in Brixham in days gone by. No traffic intrudes upon the scene to create noise and pollution and life in the town seems ordered and at peace with itself. However, it should also be remembered that there was also poverty and poor housing for many.

A fascinating feature of Brixham, and reputedly 600 year old, the Coffin House attracts hundreds of tourists each year. It is believed that its peculiarly-shaped structure was an inevitable outcome determined by the size of the site on which it was built at the bottom of Temperance Steps. There is a fascinating story handed down through the centuries which avows that a certain Dick Rounsell wanted to marry the daughter of Captain John Tuckham, a prominent Brixham fisherman. The captain, who opposed the match, told the suitor that he would rather see his daughter in a coffin. Some time later the daughter disappeared only to be found in the odd shaped house which Rounsell had built. Facing the fact that he had been outwitted the captain relented and allowed the marriage to take place. The locality became known as Ostend from the Flemish community that lived there and which is mentioned in the Parish Rates Book in the early 1700s.

20 – Grand Hotel

Grandly established for over sixty years on the high ground overlooking Brixham harbour, the Northcliffe Hotel was the principal social meeting place for the town. Here a multitude of association and club dinners and functions were held each year. Standing proud on the hilltop overlooking the harbour with excellent views east, south and west, the Northcliffe Hotel commanded an impeccable panoramic prospect.

Although the building could never be lauded for the grandeur of its architecture, its appeal lay in its lack of ostentation, its rare blend of informality and propriety, and cordiality mixed with courtesy. Once inside, a friendly aura of welcome was instantly experienced by everyone and reflected in a host of happy smiling faces. The Northcliffe was indeed the focus for Brixham's whirl of social engagements.

It was owned and run by Mrs Silley and her two daughters, Rose and Dorothea, as a family concern. But in 1953, Rose was enobled by marrying one of the guests, Cecil O'Bryen Fitzmaurice, Viscount of Kirkwall, Baron of Dechmont, the Eighth Earl of Orkney, thus making her the Countess of Orkney.

Joan Longhurst (née Reeves) and Charlie Boone were former employees and remember the Northcliffe with affection. All proprieties were carefully observed, 'White jackets at lunchtime and black tails for evening dinner.' Mrs Silley would expect nothing less than perfection from her staff.

Among many regular patrons was Maurice Scott, Governor of the Fiji Islands, novelist A.W. Mason, famous for *The Four Feathers*, Sir Malcolm Campbell and his son Donald, and Colonel Bedington who set out to sail the South China seas in Brixham-crewed trawler.

Following the retirement of Mrs Silley and its subsequent sale the hotel's service and efficiency rapidly deteriorated. In the passage of time this was followed by a cessation of business and later, the abandonment of the premises. Seizing their opportunity, squatters then occupied the building until finally a huge fire utterly destroyed it.

In 1996 a decision was made to demolish the burnt-out shell and the accompanying picture shows it as a mass of rubble. A sad and sorrowful end indeed to its lifetime of gaiety and grandeur, and the end of an era in Brixham's social history.

Above: *The Northcliffe Hotel standing on its clifftop site.*

Right: *Hotel staff, Sid Thomas, Elsie Caunter, Joan Reeves and Charlie Boone, 1940s.*

Top: *The spacious hotel dining room.* Above: *The Northcliffe's imposing frontage.*

A sad picture. Here on this demolition site, once stood the Northcliffe Hotel.

Brixham Hotelier's Fancy Dress Party, 1964. Those present include Betty Higgins, Rose Connabier, Bill Roberts, Mr and Mrs F. Pearce, Mary Murrell, Eve Bailey, Mrs and Mrs J. Phillips.

Mrs Joan Roach, 1967 Chairman of the Brixham Hotels Association, being welcomed at the Imperial Hotel by the President of the Torquay Hotels Association Mr Vernon Duker.

Among the many regular patron associations which held their dinners and social events at the Northcliffe was the Brixham Hotels Association. The picture shows some of the members at their 1965 annual dinner. Among those in the 1965 group are: Mr F. Pearce (Chairman), Mrs V. Pearce, Mrs A. Roach (President Elect), Mr A. Roach, Mr and Mrs W. Bailey, Mr F. Connabier (President), Mrs Connabier, Mr W. Saxton (Clerk to the Council), Mrs Saxton.

HM Queen Elizabeth II meets the people of Brixham, 1988.

21 – Brixham People Remembered

Wherever a place may be, how beautiful or spectacular its location, or how illustrious its history, its real heart lies in the people who live there. Brixham is fortunate to have a long and interesting place in the history of Devon and, indeed, the nation, and its people can take pride in this. This chapter contains many photographs of people taken at a variety of events and activities in the more recent past that help to bring into focus everyday aspects of the life of the town.

A CARING COMMUNITY

One test of society is to consider its care of the elderly and infirm. Brixham enjoys a good reputation in these matters and here we look at just one aspect of this, the work of Laywell House.

Brixham is justly proud of Laywell House, a Residential Home for the elderly. It is unique in several ways. This fine manor house and extensive garden was given by the late Mrs Hay-Matthey in 1958 to be used for the care of those in Brixham and Dartmouth whose age and frailty makes it impossible for them to continue living at home. The need for this was made known a year or so previously by the Brixham Old People's Welfare Committee. With this most generous gift there was, from the start, a total commitment shown by local people to provide the best care and service that was humanly possible. The administration of it was to be performed by voluntary helpers, unpaid, and chosen by election from local service and benevolent societies.

And from this there evolved a non-profit making concept that led to Charitable Status. Running costs have always been high. First there was the adaptation of a domestic house into a residential home for upwards of 36 residents, a costly business helped by donations of beds and soft furnishings.

There followed over succeeding years continual improvements and additions in connection with modernisation. Gardeners worked to provide a large vegetable garden to supply the

Laywell House.

A group of Laywell staff in 1995 celebrating the 50th anniversary of VE Day. Those present include Cynthia Maunder, Margaret Morris, Liz Urand, Audrey Shaw, Brenda Sims, Shiela Timblin, George Hayman, Gladys Hayman, Bill Maunder, Sharon Petherick, and matron Jennifer Murray.

residents with fresh vegetables. The lounge windows open out to a terrace and spacious flat lawn where residents could sit out on summer days looking beyond the flowers to the hills across the valley. The income from residents had to be supplemented and some thirty years ago there was formed the Friends of Laywell, a fund-raising charity. Local people supported this well. Its committee organise monthly lotteries, coffee mornings, cheese and wine evenings, etc.

Participation extends beyond Brixham to Kingswear where there is also an enthusiastic band of supporters. Hard work and handsome legacies have enabled there now to be a stable and satisfactory reserve of funds. This is necessary and has to be maintained to cope with unexpected emergencies and to be able to face whatever further calls are made for expanding services.

Living conditions play a large part in ensuring happiness. The spacious finely proportioned lounges stand as originally planned. The comfortable and well furnished chairs, the practical lighting and controlled heating are especially appreciated. Elderly people in particular do not

take kindly to being removed to hospital for temporary or minor illnesses and the 'new' extension has a small ward so that this can be prevented.

There are very few rules: personal freedom is uppermost. Relatives and friends are welcomed as are car trips for visits to the countryside and to children and grandchildren. Residents keep small pieces of personal furniture in their rooms. There is a separate smoking room and television lounge, and all rooms are on show at the Open Day held in mid-summer.

There is a very popular Gala Day attended by many well-wishers; the matron and Friends of Laywell jointly arrange the day. A local personality declares the Day open and the British Legion Band plays on the lawn where there are stalls and sideshows. Special encouragement is given to displays by school children. And when all the flags and bunting have been taken down and the cream teas eaten, the crowds depart happy and proud that Brixham has such a caring place. They know too that the residents are in the good hands of skilled nursing staff amongst whom there is a continuity of service.

Left: *An open day at Laywell House.*

Right: *One of Laywell's oldest residents, Miss Stubbs, celebrates her 90th birthday with her carers Valerie Wickson and Daphne Clements.*

Forty years ago the gift of the Home by Mrs Hay-Matthey and the vision of Brixham People combined with their industry, ensured that Laywell had a solid foundation on which the present-day Laywell rests. As more people now survive into old age it is comforting to know that places such as Laywell exist.

In many ways, Laywell is a landmark to them, a tribute to their spirit, and a tribute also to the town of Brixham.

SCHOOL LIFE

As with care of the elderly, the proper education of young people is paramount in building a healthy society. Brixham's many opportunities for education among the young (and for the not so young!) provide a solid base for further education.

The accompanying photographs provide a taste of school life in times gone by.

Pupils of the National Girl's School in Bolton Street in 1934. Included are Doreen Burley, Nora Light, Molly Low, Phylis Partridge, Faith Nowel, Bertha Foster, Joan Richardson, Sylvia Davis, Thelma Jake, Mary Blackam, Margaret Thomas, Lorna Barrow, Joan Hannaford, Joyce Smith, Joan Reeves, Joan Cooksley, Joyce Dalton, Phylis Bartlett, Betty Watt, Mabel Doble, Audrey Braziere, Helen Turvey, Joan Turvey, Eileen Mutte, Betty Williams.

A children's party in Mrs Binham's garden in New Road in 1953 to celebrate the Coronation of Queen Elizabeth. Among those in the photograph are Ian and Janet Endicott, Peter Wallis, John Longhurst and the Rickard sisters.

A group of Junior Pupils of St Peter's Church of England School in 1955. Miss Quirk (standing centre). Back Row l-r: Jennifer Stanford, Judy Caunter, Sandra King, Jean Dodgson, Susan Hellier, Anne Binham, Christine Campion, Jane Abbot. Front Row: John Pedrick, Peter Phillips, Brindley Parker, Colin Harris, Colin Sherritt, Alan McInally, John Longhurst, David Maddick.

Some of the pupils of Grammercy School, Brixham in 1959. The Principal of the school was Miss Findieson. Among the group are the following - Ivor Lynn, Madeline Saxton, Patricia Brewer, Simon Wright, Richard Packham, Richard Brown, Chris Roach, Rita Putt, Stephen Bower, Colin Bower, Coleen Cole, George Cole and Elizabeth Pearson

GUIDES AND SCOUTS

The introduction of youth movements which encouraged society between young people came at the end of the Victorian period. The Boys' Brigade, Sea Scouts, Scouts and Girl Guides each have had long and significant impact on the youth of Brixham. Nevertheless all of these movements have had to evolve with society, and the Girl Guides particularly has successfully incorporated the major shift that has come about in the role women play in life today.

The 4th Brixham Brownies in 1973 off on a Pack holiday to the Scilly Isles.

A Brixham Guides group in 1976. Among them are: Linda Phillips, Lorraine Collier, Alison Thomas, Sue Diton, Kerry Williams, Jennifer ?, Debbie Cook, ? Meredith, Jackie ? (now Passmore), Michelle Ewing, Karen Ganicott, Vanessa ?, Janet Lanyon, Carol Meredith, Janet Phillips.

ALL GOING SWIMMINGLY

The Brixham Swimming and Life-Saving Society was formed in 1928 with the purpose of teaching the town's children to swim and thus ultimately to save lives, and throughout the years that aim has remained unchanged.

During the early period, experienced swimmers would stand shivering in the cold waters of Shoalstone pool instructing dozens of equally chilly youngsters. It was indeed a thankless and unpopular task but they did their best.

As the demand from parents for better facilities for teaching increased, so did the need for a heated indoor pool. However for this they needed both money and a suitable site. Letters appeared in the local papers exhorting townspeople to support the project. In the process of time a site at Astley Park was offered and, thus encouraged, aid and subscriptions from various sources followed. Then came offers of free labour by contractors, cost-only materials from local tradesmen began to arrive, local organisations and individuals arranged money-raising functions, and gradually the funds began to flow in.

There is an old saying 'Don't wait for your ship to come in – row out and meet it,' and this in effect is what the members did. They were not prepared to sit back like Mr Micawber and 'wait for something to turn up,' but combined their efforts and energies and set to work to build a heated pool themselves with voluntary labour, and with materials often generously donated free of charge.

By 1972 they had partly constructed a skeleton of a building which gave sufficient cover to excavate the actual pool area inside. This was a mammoth job whereby hundreds of tons of earth and stone had to be moved and carried. Even non-members with various trades and professions came to sweat and strain, their only reward calloused hands and aching backs.

It would be impossible to list the names of everyone who played a part but mention should be made of a few who made a major contribution to the finished construction. Among these are Albert Hoyle, Graham Fellowes, John Pope (Secretary), Vic Tomlin (Chairman), Freda Evans (Treasurer) and members of the Brixham Soroptomists, Round Table and Rotary clubs.

Brixham's heated swimming pool was finished by 6 January 1975 and the official opening performed by the Duke and Duchess of Kent, in June 1975, who also presented Life Memberships to long-standing members of the club.

Some indication of the difference a heated pool made to club membership is evidenced by numbers enrolled. In the 1930s membership was around 200. After the opening of the pool, that number jumped to 1200.

The outdoor bathing pool, Brixham c.1955.

The new indoor pool as it was in 1972, partly constructed.

Brixham Opening Dip in 1924. Those present include Phyllis Smith, ? Light, Eileen Mutter, Eileen Smith, Violet Palmer, Joyce Williams, Betty James, Mr Janes (Master), Joyce Davies, Marion Potter, Nancy Kitto, Sylvia~ Rollings, Freda Potter, Marjorie Munday, Joan James, Joan Bickford, Connie Polyblank, Alice Barrett, Mary Dickers, Jessie Bond, Sonny Mead, Elsie Harris, John Creese, Alec Geddes, Nancy Price, Sam Price (Master). The photograph was taken at Fishcombe Beach, the shed provided by Mr Potter a local builder.

On the occasion of the opening of the new heated pool in June 1975 when life memberships were awarded to Albert Hoyle, John Pope, Freda Evans and Graham Fellowes. The photograph above shows Albert Hoyle being presented with his certificate by the Duke of Kent. In the photograph (right) the Duchess of Kent shakes hands with John Pope before his presentation.

A few junior members of the Brixham Swimming Club taken inside the new heated swimming pool in 1977. Top Row l-r: Kevin Dart, Andrew Young, John Alberici, Paul Alberici, Linda Criddle, Janet Clark. Front Row: Nicola Thomas, Sally Alberici, Karen Thomas, Irene Bradfield, Julie Pope, Rachael Munnings, Andrew Heard.

CARNIVAL TIME

Many, many years ago there was a period when Brixham developed into two distinct communities partitioned at the point where Raeburn Road crosses to Burton Street, dividing Higher Brixham from Lower Brixham. Here stood a Great Gate allowing access from one side to the other, at which a toll of one and a half pence was demanded from the Higher Brixham folk who wished to go down to Lower Brixham to sell their produce. In fact there still survives 'Great Gate House' close by.

The distinction between the two areas came about through the occupations of their inhabitants; whereas Lower Brixham became known as Fishtown, Higher Brixham (St Marys), because of its farming community, became Cowtown.

The Great Gate has of course long gone and any social division between the two communities has simply developed into good-humoured raillery. From this there has evolved the Cowtown Carnival whereby a group of friends formed a committee to raise money for local charities. Over the years and especially since 1977, the Cowtown Carnival, stimulated and encouraged

by its Mayor, Chairman and Committee, has raised and donated many thousands of pounds to deserving causes.

The photographs following provide an indication of the fun and frivolity enjoyed during the carnival.

A carnival float in 1976 with the theme 'Mice in a Windmill in Old Amsterdam'.

Carnival Time

Brixham Brownies' float 'Bluebells' won first prize in 1972.

Brixham Brownies and 'Rose Garden in 1975.

Carnival Time

This colourful troupe gave themselves the title 'Humphry and Friends in 1977.

Left and below: *Carnival scenes.*

Carnival Time

A fruity collection of Carnival revellers.

Camelot comes to Cowtown Carnival.

LIFT UP YOUR VOICE

Shakespeare's Orsino in *Twelfth Night* declared 'If music be the food of love – play on.' Perhaps if he had heard the melodious harmony of the Brixham Orpheus Male Voice Choir he might have changed it to 'sing on', for over the years the quality of their vocal renderings have been nationally and internationally recognised and honoured. This is evidenced by the many invitations they receive to sing at festivals and concerts, not only in this country but abroad. Additionally, the bonds forged with visiting choirs from such nations as Germany, Holland, the USA and the Soviet Union place Brixham firmly on the global map, and these gentlemen of musical talent have become Britain's ambassadors to appreciative audiences in many lands.

While the choir undoubtedly owe their success to the excellence and unity of its many voices, signal honours must also be accorded to those who have worked with the choir over the years: musical director Eddie Phillips, and the piano accompanyists Margaret Pitman and Daphne Murphy, secretary Ray Jago and Chairman Stan Gregory, along with an army of ladies who support and sustain the choir's financial commitments with constant fund raising events.

Brixham Orpheus Male Voice Choir, 1996, with ladies of the support group and musical director Eddie Phillips and accompanyist Daphne Murphy. Among those present are: Phineas Barnes, Ellis Boulton, Dennis Crockett, Bill Hannaby, John Green, Derek Hill, John Morris, Barry Pike, Neil Price, Roy Silman, Gerry Simmons, Carl Ansell, Ernie Ashford, Ron Barrington, Bernard Partridge, Harold Dutton, Peter Goodier, Bob Hughes, Richard Wills, Alec Milsom, Gordon Moore, Cecil Tomlin, Clive Archer, Ray Blood, David Brown, Harry Couchman, Ray Jago, Stan Gregory, Cliff Hamer, Frank Hartland, Stan Mitchelmore, Stan Hodge, Alex Hutcheon, Don Thompson, Brian Tucker, Ernie Widger, Frank Burley, Oscar Edwards, Austin Guy, Hugh Hamilton, Paddy Paddock, Bill Pocock, Henry Tribble, Vernon Tucker, Derek Walker, John Yolland, Geoff Howells. Ladies support group: Dot Blood, Cynthia Burrington, Barbara Dutton, Marjorie Edwards, Norma Franklyn, Olive Green, Marion Gregory, Joan Goodier, Marie Hannaby, Joan Hodge, Barbara Hutcheon, Audrey Jago, Carolyn Morgan, Jean Phillips, Frances Silman, Shirley Thompson, Janet Tomlin, Jean Tribble, Betty Tucker, Gwenda Tucker, Pat Walker, Betty Widger, Joy Yolland.

Brixham Orpheus Male Voice Choir, 1955. Back Row l-r: *David Lovegrove, Tom Featherstone, Russel Pine, Bert Dalley, J. Broth, Len Lear, Albert Beaumont, H. Dickenson.* Middle Row: *Harry Morey, H. Ash, John Youlden, Sam Hazelwood, N. Eccleston, W. Stevens, George Stapleston, Albert Moxey, Ernie Ashford.* Front row: *Alf Morgan, Harold Macmasters, Tom Snell, Len Pitman, Margaret Pitman (accompanyist), William E. Trant (conductor), G.G. Bradshaw, R.F. Buley, Sam. T. Robertson, A. Ken Jones.*

Brixham Harvest of the Sea Choir. This was an interdenominational choir where members were drawn from churches in the town. They travelled throughout the Westcountry in the 1970s and 1980s giving gospel services. The picture includes back row l-r: Chivers, Tuckett, Penn, Chivers, Partridge, Friend, Meaker, Millsom, Banberry, Pillar, Bond, Pillar, Taylor, Binham, Robertson, Myers, Sharp, Pocock, Hingston. Front row: *Stevens, Hazel, Phillips, Bywater, Clarke, Hughes, Kirk, Phillips, Jones, Gregory, Worth. The choir was disbanded in 1988.*

TREADING THE BOARDS

The Brixham Operatic and Dramatic Society (BOADS) was born out of a popular concert party known as the 'Orange Bubbles' in the 1920s, directed by Ralph Bartlett. Growing in strength the group changed its name to Brixham Operatic Society, rehearsing its shows in Miss Bovey's school on Cavern Hill. The first production was 'The Pearl Fisherman' followed by 'Merrie England' in 1929. It was this production that brought Brixham man Bill Smardon into the limelight going on to a forty year association with the society that also involved his wife Marjorie and their daughter Isabelle, now Isabelle Barker, and with him becoming its chairman.

During these early days the shows became vast affairs, drawing audience from far and near with, among other shows, 'The Mikado' and 'Iolanthe'. In 1930 they entered a new era when they engaged a professional producer, Jeffery Snelson. He later married Margaret Warren the choreographer of the 1946 show 'The Belle of New York'.

Memories and anecdotes abound. In 1935 the society staged 'The Desert Song', the scenery sent directly to Brixham from the stage at Drury Lane. It was about this time that the dramatic section was born, with familiar names such as Beryl Decent and Bill Jordain at the forefront of the early productions. The dramatic section went on to win several cups at the Festival Theatre, Paignton, with Frank Blenkin, Nancy Duncan and Myra Risk playing a variety of dramatic roles.

It was at this point that Snelson's artistic talents were revealed to the full, for with the advent of war it was impossible to get scenery and he decided to make his own, creating the most spectacular sets ever seen in the area. Several of his initial ideas can be seen at the Brixham Museum.

BOADS' popularity continued and in 1953 they were the first in Devon to stage 'Annie Get Your Gun'. The cost of the shows was only met by frantic fund raising. Smardon's shop in Bolton Street sold the theatre tickets, and for 'Annie Get Your Gun' people queued at two in the morning to get seats. Even during the matinée queues formed for the evening performances. In those days most of the lead parts were taken by Brixham people, among them Ron Packham, Isabelle and Derrick Barker, Frank Bowles, Nora Bovey, Megan Way, Joan O'Nions and Nettie Fowler. Even the Cowtown Mayor John Beer appeared as one of Mr Snow's children in 'Carousel'. One of the most memorable productions was the 'Merry Widow' in 1959.

By the 1950s and into the 60s as many as three productions were being staged each year including the successful 'South Pacific' in 1961.

Known as the Blackhand Gang, a team of twelve stalwarts worked hard with the scene

'Merrie England', 1929.

VISIT OF H.M.S. COMUS.

PROGRAMME OF GRAND VARIETY CONCERT

Arranged and presented by Jay Seele

IN THE TOWN HALL, BRIXHAM, ON FRIDAY, JULY 20th, 1928,

Commencing at 7.30 p.m.

PART I.

1. There will NOT BE the usual Opening Chorus

2. Our LEN, being in the Diplomatic Corps, has kept his Item a secret

3. A.B. CLAYTON will tell us of the " Pigtail of Li Fang Fu "

4. It is time you heard LITTLE WINNIE, who will " Echo " and then sing of " Fairings "

5. DR. R. B. THOMPSON, complete with Kilt, reminds us of the old days, and gives us his reason for being a " Kiltie "

6. CYRIL will tell you how he spends his Friday Nights

7. JAY SEELE, the Curate with a Smile, will possibly speak of his Parishioners
   (This item is to give the Artists a respite)

8. JONATHAN SMALL hopes to " Sprout," and please do not throw cabbages, he is young and tender

9. HUMOROUS SKETCH "A Turn of Leave"
   L.S. SCHWEEN   A.B. THORMILLEY
   A.B. HALE   L.S. FLETCHER

-An Interval of about Ten Minutes.

PART II.

9. Our SAILOR LADDIES will jazz a tune or two

10. LEONARD, still diplomatic, refuses to have his item printed

11. CYRIL & JAY will, by special request, recall the " Flying of Time " (Oh, where is our Ralph ? he does it so well !)

12. DR. R. B. THOMPSON will sing of his " Loving Highland Lassie " (Note the Glengarry)

13. A.B. CLAYTON will warble of his darling " Two Eyes of Blue "

14. WINNIE, getting excited, will tell you how she loves her boatman, and then, possibly, of, an experience " Under the Moon "

15. CYRIL will again " bare his soul "

16. JONATHAN SMALL (the doubting tar of H.M.S. Neptune, 1908) will again grow expansive

17. And then we shall close with HIGHER DRAMA of a most seriousque nature (they all are) will be presented to you. (Do not be frightened at the sound of firearms)

Cast :

Countess Notsomuchovit	An Adventuress	Winifred Murley
Derek Despard	Her Accomplice	Jay Seele
The Earl of Dulditch	Just an Earl	Cyril Hoskins
Lady Ermyntrude	His Daughter	Miss S. Drew
Claud Carisbroke	Her Lover	Mr. Walter Mitchell
Musical Thrumps	by	Mr. Howard Partridge
Scenic Effects	by	Our Leonard

" GOD SAVE THE KING "

At the Piano - - MR. HOWARD PARTRIDGE

During the Interval, Musical Selections will be rendered by the Magnatone.

A programme of a variety concert held at the Town Hall, Brixham, in 1928. Artistes in the performance included Winifred Murley, Jay Seele, Cyril Hoskins, Miss S. Drew, Walter Mitchell, and Howard Partridge. The programme was printed by Messrs S.G. Goad of Brixham.

changes. They included Bert Lidstone, Fred Moxley, Emps Buley and Bill Smardon. But change was in the air, with pantomime creeping into the already busy programme.

Came 1963 and the end of an era with the production of 'The Pyjama Game'. After thirty dedicated years Jeffery Snelson decided now was the time to leave BOADS, and the same year also saw the departure of his friend Bill Smardon. But all was not lost for into the breach stepped Peter

Clapham, a young and enthusiastic man who had appeared in earlier BOADS productions. His first show was Noel Coward's 'Bitter Sweet', with Isabelle Barker singing the leading role as she did in many of the shows.

Peter Clapham's attention to detail was just as thorough as Jeffery Snelson's, for everything had to be meticulously correct. 'Bittersweet' required technical expertise and Wally Robins who used to teach at Furzeham School joined the backstage

'South Pacific' 1961.

'Brigadoon' 1967.

'Waltzes from Vienna'.

'Half a Sixpence', 1968

'Perchance to Dream', 1980

'The Sound of Music, 1977.

'Liza', and a cast of forty-two, 1975.

gang to construct solid and intricate sets. Ralph Jones and Ted Bevin also joined at this time, the latter getting roped in to go on stage as well.

Isabelle Barker remembers that the actors and actresses would be called on to do many different things and, even though she herself would be playing many of the leading roles, she also had to sweep the stage.

In 1965 came 'Marietta', in 1966 'Gypsy Love', and a year later 'Brigadoon'. It was around 1967 that Tony Burke joined the backstage team and later married Brixham girl Ann Beer. In 1968 the society's superb show 'Half a Sixpence' was received with enormous enthusiasm.

While the dramatic section was busy putting on two plays a year, the society continued with lavish shows such as 'Waltzes from Vienna' in 1971, helped by Maurice Hemming's working on scenery painting, while his wife Stella was pianist. The expenses were enormous but, despite this, the BOADS bought its own rehearsal hall in the old Catholic Church after its move to its new site in New Road. Although the new acquisition was just a shell, carpenters Ralph Jones and Ted Bevin soon knocked it into shape.

'Waltzes from Vienna' proved to be one of the most popular shows of BOADS's many productions for it provided a galaxy of colour and music, and in which Isabelle Barker with her magnificent voice justified the lead.

The 1950s and 1960s were considered by some to be a Golden Age in the modern theatre. Other members involved at this time were familiar Brixham names: Betty Higgins, Nancy Morris, John Beer and Ron Packham.

Another first for Brixham was the staging of the popular musical of the time 'Paint your Wagon', with the leading man Malcolm Jordain as Ben Runson. In 1973 under Torbay Borough Council the Town Hall was refurbished, with 300 plush tip-up seats and the stage being improved. Before these changes, in the thirties, they crammed in as many chairs as possible and even scores of fish boxes to sit on.

In the seventies 'The Vagabond King' and 'Annie Get Your Gun' revived, with Jill Farrant coming on the scene to produce 'Viva Mexico' and 'The Sound of Music'. Ron Packham played Von Trapp, Jan Thomas, Maria, and Isabelle Barker the Mother Abbess.

There was another winning production in 1979 with 'The Song of Norway', and in 1980 'The Wizard of Oz' was produced in pantomime style. One of the later musicals 'My Fair Lady', presented in 1989, introduced the talented young 16-year-old Samantha Lynham from Stoke Fleming playing the lead as Eliza Doolittle.

Despite a few setbacks BOADS can look back over the last eighty years with pride and affection, knowing that their amalgam of keen and proficient amateurs allied to the directive of stage professionals can and has produced musical productions of the highest standard and of which Brixham can be justifiably proud.

Hellevoetsluis

The people of Brixham welcome William Prince of Orange in 1688.

Brixham

22 – Twinning

It is perhaps inevitable that when the vogue for twinning English towns with those on the Continent began in the 1970s, Brixham should look to the Netherlands for a partner. The association of the town with Holland, through its connection with the landing of Prince William, makes such a twinning partnership all the more meaningful. The photographs below record a celebratory occasion on the twinning of Brixham with Hellevoetsluis in 1982.

A smiling Queen in Brixham, July 1988.

23 – A Royal Visit - 300 Years On

The visit to Brixham of Her Majesty Queen Elizabeth II to commemorate the tercentenary of the landing of William, Prince of Orange, in 1688 was one of the highlights of the town's long heritage. The day, 21 July 1988, began quietly enough with just a handful of early sightseers who had staked their claim at the barriers on the quay as early as 6am armed with chairs, cushions, flasks of coffee and snacks.

The inner harbour was a rare sight indeed, for all boats had been removed to the outer area. With no breeze disturbing the sleeping water, the satin surface mirrored every hue and form of the surrounding hillsides. The only signs of activity were a few council workmen sweeping the streets and, of course, squadrons of seagulls on the wing.

As the morning wore on, however, pavements rapidly filled with spectators forming grandstand terraces and soon every vantage point, every window and verandah was occupied. Thousands of people, not only from Brixham but from all parts of Devon, had arrived. An air of excitement and the cheerful sound of chatter filled the air.

The threat of terrorist attack brought teams of security personnel who investigated every possible nook and cranny where danger might lurk.

Spectators around the quay were surprised to see manhole covers being removed and from their gaping depths men emerge after checking the tunnels and passages below.

In the streets, gaily dressed crowds waved a mass of union flags to create a sea of red, white and blue. Brixham's patriotism was clearly unbounded.

At the appointed time, the royal barge, escorted by the Torbay lifeboat arrived at Brixham pier, and the monarch, dressed in emerald green, accompanied by Prince Philip and the present Prince Willem of Orange, was received by the Mayor and Mayoress Alderman Denis Reid and Mrs Reid and the Lord Lieutenant, the Earl of Morley.

Not even the rain falling from a grey sky later in the morning dampened the spirits of the people, and the events surrounding the ceremony, including the unveiling of a commemorative plaque at the harbourside, were greeted with great jubilation. The following photographs are an important historical record of this momentous occasions and a reminder of an event which sums up Brixham's sense of pride in her long and illustrious history.

The royal party enjoy the re-enactment of William's historic landing.

A modern day Prince William, played by actor Roger Rees, provided an re-enactment of the arrival in 1688.

Prince Philip stops to talk to a flag-waving spectator.

Despite the rain the Queen enjoys her day.

The Queen and her entourage arrive at the statue of William watched by enthusiastic crowds.

The Queen unveils the new plaque commemorating the tercentenary of William's landing at Brixham in 1688 watched (left) by a smiling mayor, Dennis Reid, and (right) by the Earl Morley, Lord Lieutenant of the County.

Her Majesty Queen Elizabeth II at the statue of her royal predecessor.

24 Harbourside Scenes

Above: *Fishermen's cottages, fish lofts and cellars crowd above the harbour in this late-nineteenth-century view.*

Right: *A decline in the fishing industry fuelled by a general depression following the Great War is evidenced in this photograph of an almost empty harbour seen in the mid 1920s.*

Left: *An early postcard view of the harbour and the statue of William of Orange, erected in the year this photograph was taken, 1891.*

Left: *An unusual view from west Brixham across to Torquay and Berry Head, from a watercolour by F.J. Widgery c.1920.*

Below: *A Valentine & Sons postcard view of Brixham looking into the harbour c.1920.*

Another postcard view of the harbour, c.1900.

Index

THE BOOK OF BRIXHAM

Dart, Kevin 103
Davies, Joyce 102
Davis, Sylvia 97
Decent, Beryl 109
Dewdney, Harold 37
Dibley, Brian 41
Dickenson, H. 108
Dickers, Mary 102
Disney, John 48
Diton, Sue 100
Dobbins, Thomas 13
Doble, Mabel 97
Dodgson, Jean 98
Drew, S. 110
Duker, V. 93
Duncan, Nancy 109
Dunn (family) 48
Dunn, Geoff 49
Dutton, Barbara 107
Dutton, Harold 107
Dyer, Bill 51

Ecclestone, N. 108
Edey, M. 55
Edmonds, Sid 51
Edwards, C. 65
Edwards, D. 49
Edwards, Marjorie 107
Edwards, Oscar 107
Edwards, P. 55
Edwards, W. 49
Elliot, Richard Couch 85
Ellis (family) 41
Endicott, Ian 98
Endicott, Janet 98
Evans, Freda 100, 102
Evans, Wayne 50
Ewing, Michelle 100

Foster (family) 33
Foster, Bertha 97
Fowler, Nettie 109
Fox, Jim 77
Fradd (family) 48, 60
Franklin, A. 52
Franklyn, Norma 107
Fraser, Mary E. 27
Freed, M. 52
Friend (family) 108

Gagg, Doris 78
Gagg, Mary 77, 78
Gagg, Norman 77
Ganicott, Karen 100
Gardiner, T. 49

Geddes, Alec 102
Gibbs, F. 49
Gibbs, William 59
Gibson, S.C. 49
Gibson, S.G. 49
Gilbert, Sir Humphrey 25
Gill, J. 62
Goddard, J. 55
Goddard, W. 55
Godfrey, D. 85
Goodier, Joan 107
Goodier, Peter 107
Goodson, Hugh 77
Goodson, Sir Alfred 62
Gowman, Harry 37
Graham, R. 52
Green, F. 49
Green, John 107
Green, Olive 107
Greenaway, D. 52
Gregory 60, 108
Gregory, Marion 107
Gregory, Stan 107
Griffiths, Taff 51
Grontenrath, John 51
Guy (family) 60
Guy, Austin 107

Hall, S.H. 70
Hamer, Cliff 107
Hamilton, Hugh 107
Hannaby, Bill 107
Hannaby, Marie 107
Hannaford, Joan 97
Harding (family) 60
Harper, Terry 52
Harrington, Mike 48
Harris, Colin 98
Harris, E. 68
Harris, Elsie 102
Hartland, Frank 107
Harvey, N. 52
Hatherley, E.G. 49
Hatherley, F. 33
Hatherley, George 49
Hatherley, H. 33
Hayman, George 96
Hayman, Gladys 96
Hay-Matthey 69, 95, 97
Hazel (family) 108
Hazlewood, Sam 108
Heard, Andrew 103
Hellier, Susan 98
Helly, Russell 49
Heron, A. 85

Higgins, Betty 93, 113
Hill, Derek 107
Hingston 108
Hingston, Brian 48
Hodge, Joan 107
Hodge, Stan 107
Hogg, Miss A.M. 23, 62
Hogg, Revd John Roughton 23
Holding, John 50
Hollingworth, D. 52
Holloway (family) 60
Hook, Stafford 70
Horrocks, J. 55
Hoskins (family) 60
Hoskins, Cyril 110
How, R. 52
Howells, Geoff 107
Hoyle, Albert 49, 51, 100, 102
Hughes 108
Hughes, Bob 107
Hutcheon, Alex 107
Hutcheon, Barbara 107

Israel, L. 55
Ivey, Bill 50
Ivey, Steven 50

Jackman, T. 33
Jackson, Walter 51
Jago, A. 52
Jago, Audrey 107
Jago, Ray 107
Jake, Thelma 97
James, Betty 102
James, Joan 102
Janes (family) 102
Jarrowson, Andrew 52
Jenkins, Maldwyn 51
Johns, C. 65
Johnson 60
Jones 60, 108
Jones, A. Ken 108
Jones, Ralph 113
Jordain (family) 60
Jordain, Bill 109
Jordain, Malcolm 113
Junker, Jan 55
Jury, Ken 78
Jury, Mary 77, 78

Kennar, G. 49
Kent, C. 49
King, Jonathon 50
King, Sandra 98
Kirk (family) 108

ALSO AVAILABLE IN THE SERIES

The Book of Addiscombe • Various
Book of Bampton • Caroline Seward
Book of Bickington • Stuart Hands
The Book of Blandford Forum • Various
The Book of Brixham • Frank Pearce
The Parish Book of Cerne Abbas • Vale & Vale
The Book of Chittlehampton • Various
The Book of Constantine • Moore & Trethowan
The Book of Cornwood and Lutton • Various
The Book of Creech St Michael • June Small
The Book of Cullompton • Various
The Book of Grampound with Creed • Bane & Oliver
The Book of Hayling Island and Langstone • Rogers
The Book of Helston • Jenkin with Carter
The Book of Hemyock • Clist & Dracott
The Book of High Bickington • Avril Stone
The Book of Ilsington • Dick Wills
The Book of Lamerton • Ann Cole and Friends
Lanner, A Cornish Mining Parish • Scharron Schwartz & Roger Parker
The Book of Loddiswell • Various
The Book of Lustleigh • Tim Hall
The Book of Manaton • Various
The Book of Meavy • Pauline Hemery
The Book of Morchard Bishop • Jeff Kingaby
The Book of Minehead with Alcombe • Binding & Stevens
The Book of North Newton • Robins & Robins
The Book of Pimperne • Compiled by Jean Coull
The Book of Plymtree • Tony Eames
The Book of Porlock • Dennis Corner
Postbridge – The Heart of Dartmoor • Reg Bellamy
The Book of Priddy • Various
The Book of Rattery • Various
The Book of South Stoke with Midford • Various
South Tawton and South Zeal with Sticklepath • Roy and Ursula Radford
The Book of Stourton Caundle • Philip Knott
The Book of Swanage • Rodney Legg
The Book of Torbay • Frank Pearce
Widecombe: Uncle Tom Cobley and All • Stephen Woods
The Book of Watchet • Compiled by David Banks
The Book of West Huntspill • Various
Widecombe-in-the-Moor • Stephen Woods
The Book of Williton • Michael Williams
Woodbury: The Twentieth Century Revisited • Roger Stokes
The Book of Woolmer Green • Various

SOME OF THE MANY FORTHCOMING TITLES IN HARDBACK

The Book of Addiscombe, Vol. II • Various
The Book of Barnstaple • Avril Stone
The Book of the Bedwyns • Various
The Book of Bideford • Peter Christie
The Book of Brampford • Various
The Book of Breage and Germoe • Stephen Polglase
The Book of Bridestowe • R. Cann
The Book of Bridport • Rodney Legg
The Book of Buckland Monachorum • Hemery
The Book of Carharrack • Various
The Book of Carshalton • Stella Wilks
The Book of Chagford • Ian Rice
The Book of Chapel-en-le-Frith • Mike Smith
*The Book of Chittlehamholt with
Warkleigh & Satterleigh* • Richard Lethbridge
The Book of Colney Heath • Bryan Lilley
*The Book of Dulverton
with Brushford, Bury & Exebridge* • Various
The Book of Dunster • Hilary Binding
The Book of Kingskerswell • Various
The Book of Lewisham Town, Lee Green and Blackheath • Various
The Book of Lulworth • Rodney Legg
The Book of Lyme Regis • Rodney Legg
The Book of Markyate • Richard Hogg
The Book of Mawnan Smith • Various
The Book of Nether Stowey • Various
The Book of Newdigate • John Callcut
The Book of Newton Abbot • Iain Rice
The Book of North Tawton • Various
The Book of Northlew with Ashbury • Various
The Book of Nynehead • Various
The Book of Pentewan • Evans and Rabjohns
The Book of Peter Tavy • Various
The Book of Princetown • Gardner-Thorpe
The Book of Publow with Pensford • Various
The Book of St Day • Annear and Mills
*The Book of Sampford Courtenay
with Honeychurch* • Stephanie Pouya
The Book of Southbourne • Rodney Legg
The Book of Staverton • Pete Lavis
The Book of Studland • Rodney Legg
The Book of Tavistock • Gerry Woodcock

For details of any of the above titles or if you are interested in writing your own community history, please contact: Community Histories Editor, Halsgrove House, Lower Moor Way, Tiverton Business Park, Tiverton, Devon EX16 6SS, England, e-mail: naomic@halsgrove.com